ALL THE PAINTINGS OF
GIOTTO
Part 1
VOLUME EIGHTEEN
in the
Complete Library of World Art

The Complete Library of World Ar

ALL THE PAINTINGS

Giotto di Bondone

OF **GIOTTO**

Part I

Text by ROBERTO SALVINI

Translated by PAUL COLACICCHI

HAWTHORN BOOKS, INC.

Publishers · New York

Manufactured in Great Britain by Jarrold & Sons Ltd, Norwich

CONTENTS

GIOTTO DI BONDONE

Life and Work

GIOTTO is known to us traditionally as the hero of a naturalistic revolution that is supposed to have broken all bonds with the Middle Ages and to have laid the foundations of modern painting. Ever since Cennino Cennini saw in Giotto the translator of art "from Greek into Latin" and ever since Ghiberti and Vasari proclaimed that Giotto had overcome the "roughness of the Greeks," art historians have insisted on stressing the revolutionary impact of his art on Byzantine tradition.

It is true that Giotto's vision of nature was distinct from the ceremonial abstraction of Byzantine painting. But this nature was still centered on man and reflected through absolute moral and religious law. Nor is the heritage of Byzantine civilization entirely lost, for the exact and hierarchical system that governs Giotto's compositions has its remote but unquestionable basis in classic Byzantine art.

Giotto's art as a whole, however, can only be understood as the epitome of the livelier tendencies of the Western Middle Ages. In contrasting to the absolute Byzantine chromaticism an equally absolute but opposed plasticity, in moving from the closed circle of Byzantine harmony to the level of dynamic composition, he was part of the whole Western tradition of Romanesque and Gothic art. Thus the heavy and inarticulate feeling for masses of Romanesque sculpture is essential to Giotto's plasticity, while his manner of composing through an interplay of tensions and distensions appears as a new interpretation of the dynamic linearity of the Gothic.

If one were to undertake a study of the artistic culture of the Middle Ages as extensive as that carried out to discover the sources of the *Divine Comedy*, one should conclude that Giotto was almost a *summa* of the representational culture of both the Western and Eastern Middle Ages, a definite synthesis of the two discordant traditions from which Italian art sprang.

Giotto was born probably in 1267 in a village in the Mugello area, called Colle di Vespignano, a few miles north of Florence. Tradition has it that his family was of peasant stock and written documents indicate that in later years he was a local landowner, but this presumably resulted from his profession rather than his inheritance.

Modern critics have repeatedly contested the conventional belief that Cimabue was Giotto's master with the theory that his style derived from the Roman School of the thirteenth century. But the fact that he clearly had a deep knowledge of the Roman School cannot rule out certain points of contact with Cimabue; these seem extremely probable both from a historical point of view and from the style of some of Giotto's early works. Nor should one forget that Cimabue worked in Rome and that Roman artists worked at his side in the Upper Church of San Francesco at Assisi.

Here, in the uppermost course of frescoes on the walls beneath the nave's first two vaults (that is to say, the third and fourth vaults in order of execution, because the basilica's pictorial decoration started from the choir and presumably continued towards the façade), one may find the earliest evidence—of a very high order—of Giotto's art. In the third vault from the choir he painted two frescoes that are outstanding in quality and novelty of expression.

These are the *Stories of Isaac* (plates 1 and 3), clearly influenced by the Roman school and Cavallini in the warmth of their colors, the statuesque character of their figures, the clear perception of space, and by Cimabue in the firmness of their contours. Such influences are at least consistent with what one may legitimately assume was Giotto's education. Cimabue's closed, almost contracted plasticity is replaced by an assured modulation of form, and the conception of space reveals Giotto's mastery and development of Cavallini's fragmentary ideas. This is shown by the perspective suggestions of the beams of the ceiling (Gioseffi). In the scene *Isaac Blessing Jacob* (plate 1), because its upper part is in better condition and therefore its architectural structure is more evident in spite of the damaged figures, one has the impression of being confronted with a sort of box inserted into the frame. The figures fill the box with a slow and rhythmic scansion, suggesting a curious feeling of detachment, even though narration is clear and the gestures sober and precise. It is as if the fresh, naturalistic drama about to be played were cloaked in the dignity of primitive myth, and sought expression through silent communion between figures as stately and solemn as ancient statues. Consequently it is perfectly natural to find the reclining Isaac (plate 3) on his Roman bed strongly evocative of ancient classic figures. The frescoes are worthy of Giotto's style; whether they can compare with those and other works which he is definitely known to have painted is a problem we shall investigate later. In another vault, Giotto painted more freely the *Stories of Joseph* (plates 16 and 18) against a background of hills.

And what a beautiful glimpse of the landscape that tree

9

on a slope in *The Slaying of Abel* (plate 10) offers us! In *The Resurrection* (plate 15), almost entirely ruined in the upper part, the sleeping soldiers are depicted with a modern sense of plasticity—one could almost say a purer geometry— which can only be found in other details of Giotto's works in *The Lamentation* (plate 11) the composition based upon several main lines converging toward the compact group in the foreground, similar to a lunette, the cross-section of the rock and the frozen flight of sorrowful angels prefigure the dominant themes of the Padua *Lamentation* (plate 143). There are also in this fresco some exchanges of glances and an elegant sobriety of gestures which we shall find again in many works by Giotto in Assisi and Padua. The chromatic intonation, warm and lively, the types of figures and the pauses in the composition certainly recall the *Stories of Isaac* but, the stately composure of the cast having been softened, the incisive linearity of certain passages becomes more obvious. Observe the first figure standing on the right; clearly, it is part of the Cimabue inheritance and indeed, if one rejected the Cimabue premise, one could never explain the tense profiles, charged with restrained energy, of the figures bending over Christ's lifeless body (plates 12 and 13). By paying attention to these details one can, and in fact should, establish a connection between Cimabue and Giotto that cannot be based merely upon a few passive residues of archaic mannerisms in Giotto's early works, but a connection that has full significance as a positive contribution by Cimabue to Giotto's new pictorial language.

But again, in *The Lamentation*, and so far as one can see through the injuries wrought by time, the figures tend to develop inside clear and well-rounded outlines, conceived with assurance. One perceives beneath them a plastic sensitivity, if not new at least re-created, a harsh, almost raw sensitivity, as compared to the gradings and modulations of relief in the *Stories of Isaac*.

Space is handled differently: it is no longer a cavity which the figures should occupy, in accordance with some formal law, but something that "emerges"—without perspective support—from the distribution of volumes, from the relationship between full and empty areas. This is practically always happening in the works in Assisi and Padua, where space is generated not so much from the relationships between a container and its contents as from the interplay and collision of masses. This principle helps to explain the lesser clarity, in terms of space, of *The Lamentation*: the point of greater limpidity is to be found in the area of the two women and the rock; it is from here that space spreads throughout the whole composition, but after this point the escalade of figures on the left becomes too steep, and as a result of this the central group is seen to float perilously close to the brink on the lower edge of the picture. Space, therefore, instead of being flat, as in the *Stories of Isaac*, a mere background for an ancient legend, becomes here part of the drama, expanding in those areas where sorrow is more deeply felt by the participants and contracting in tightly knit volumes and curves near Christ's body, the focal area of the greatest grief.

From this composition there appeared to emerge what Salmi described as "a measured, profound pathos, equally removed from Cimabue's eruptive sense of drama and from the solemn, hermetic spirit of the Master of Isaac." In fact, one can hardly blame those who doubt that if *The Lamentation* is to be accepted as the beginning of Giotto's own art, the same mind could have conceived the much more detached *Stories of Isaac*. On the other hand, the affinities are so striking in the colors as well as in the figures that one is forced to conclude that if Giotto painted *The Lamentation* no one else could have painted the two *Stories of Isaac*.

To our mind there is no need to explain such a diversity of conception between these two works—which could not have been painted over an interval of more than a few years —by claiming that Giotto interrupted his work at Assisi and returned to Rome in the intervening period. These differences are not necessarily evidence of two different phases in his formation. Considering the enormous range which he showed later, he may well have reacted differently to the various themes which struck his fancy. In any case the chronological priority should go to the *Stories of Isaac*, contrary to what some critics (Toesca, Gnudi) believe. Having arrived from Rome where to Cimabue's teachings he had added his impressions of that city's classical style of painting in the late thirteenth century and of Cavallini's frescoes in San Paolo, Giotto was confronted with the task of painting such Biblical subjects as the Isaac stories. What could have been more natural than for him to express in a more unified and dramatic form the ancient almost archaic vision inspired in him by Cavallini?

Later on, entrusted with the richer narrative contents of such themes as *Cain and Abel* and the adventure *Stories of Joseph*, and meditating perhaps for the first time over the Passion of Christ, his language became less stilted, his expression more articulate, his impetus stronger. Such expression may still appear less mature than the beautifully calibrated compositions of the *Stories of Isaac*, but in fact it implies a surprising understanding of a new world and a closer preparation for that explosion of his inventive and pictorial genius which was again set off by his coming into contact with a new subject: *The Legend of St Francis*. Longhi wrote: "The new and untouched subject of the life of St

Francis, which was then little more than fifty years old, compelled Giotto to revise entirely his attitude as well: the ancient *gravitas*, which he had brought to the Biblical and evangelistic subjects of Isaac and Christ, was no longer required. . . ." All we need add is that a first formal revision had already taken place between the solemn *Stories of Isaac* and the more stimulating subjects of the New Testament and the Passion.

A short time after their first attempts—which took place between 1290 and 1295—Giotto painted the *Crucifix* in the Church of Santa Maria Novella in Florence (plate 20). Here Christ appears in a vision of plastic equilibrium which cannot be dissociated from the sculpture of Nicola Pisano and, even more, of Arnolfo: the formalistic style of the Pisa sculptors must surely have contributed, in a broad sense, to Giotto's development. The figures of the two mourners upon the horizontal arm of the Cross have their counterparts in the *Lament* and, more important still, this panel, like the Assisi fresco, displays an obvious effort to enclose the images in a solid volumetric system within the exact and relentless boundaries of an incisive outline. At the same time the modulations of volume are achieved through *chiaroscuro* and clear design.

We come thus to *The Legend of St Francis* (plates 26–77), consisting of twenty-eight frescoes upon the lower walls of the Assisi Upper Church and presumably painted in the very last years of the thirteenth century. The master did not paint them all: his assistants' collaboration is evident throughout the cycle, and becomes dominant in the last five scenes. But the imprint of a single artistic personality is obvious throughout.

Instead of drawing from the Franciscan iconography as popularized in the third century, Giotto re-created even the most familiar scenes. This iconography had developed along the lines of an anecdotal style which derived from the discovery of some fragments of nature shining among the abstract schemes of Romanesque and Byzantine traditions. Giotto had other aims: his treatment of the legend is different not so much because it is more naturalistic in imagery and surroundings, but rather because of the spirit of simplification and order which governs it. In each narrative moment Giotto isolates the dominant note of dramatic emotion, and by focusing upon human events, appears to seek in a religious ethos the motives of man's actions. He tends to enclose each physical phenomenon of nature and man—having studied them thoroughly—into a plastic synthesis, so that each scene is made concrete within an architecture of volumes. For this particular period in Assisi the synthesis, as a compositional articulation of plastic masses, was still uncertain and intermittent, at times because the artist had not yet achieved full control over his vision but more often because the sense of the absolute was mixed with his lyrical enthusiasm for a new and unexpected revelation of the world. Dramatic rigor in short was modified by Giotto's astonishment in contemplating creation itself.

It has been recently observed, perhaps as a reaction to a long and often rambling critical tradition, that Giotto's point of view would have been exactly the opposite of that of St Francis. Indeed, the vigorous image of the Saint frescoed on the Basilica's walls shows little of the humility and ascetic fervor normally associated with the *poverello*, and his whole behavior is seen by Giotto as manly and heroic, an image that emerges from Dante's famous lines: "*Né gli gravò viltà di cor le ciglia. Regalmente sua dura intenzione || Ad Innocenzo aperse....*" ("Nor did cowardice of heart make him lower his brow. Proudly he revealed his firm resolve to Pope Innocent.")

But it is also true that the charitable *élan* which in early Franciscan literature invests every object and being in creation, enfolding miracles in an aura of tender emotion, is the source of the lyrical inspiration and religious wonder that pervade the heroic and dramatic tone of Giotto's art.

Every aspect of Giotto's representational language is related to these fundamental sources, which would quickly become apparent from an analytic study of his paintings.

His space, as we have seen in *The Lamentation*, is born from the interplay of volumes. It does not exist before them, ideally speaking, and cannot be conceived without them. The composition, meanwhile, refers constantly to a background plane, whole and impenetrable; if there is a sky, this does not envelop forms but propels them towards the foreground.

And against this background, space develops primarily from the compositional relationship between full and empty areas, at times exalting its own volumetric substance through the mysterious presence—which today would be described as unreal—of architectural "pieces" realized by a systematic breakdown of the masses. Note the two undefinable buildings in *St Francis Renouncing the World* (plate 32), which are obviously put there to set out the rhythmic plasticity of the groups of figures; of *The Ordeal by Fire* (plate 47), in which the room necessary for the movement of the participants is squeezed from the masses of the two structures. Another instance is *The Vision of the Thrones* (plate 42), in which that minimum of depth indicated by the narrow strip of land becomes hyperbolically exaggerated out of all natural proportions in the unusual spatial treatment of the concave apse, thus setting off the compact volume of the praying Saint. Finally, we have *The Expulsion of the Demons from Arezzo* (plate 44) in which the space necessary to the figure of St

Sylvester is obtained by suddenly interrupting the axial convergence of the Duomo and the walled city. Here, too, the relationship between the two buildings is not to be found in a balance of volumes in relation to a given interval but in a dynamic connection between masses which isolates the image of one man so as to heighten the spiritual drama. Notice, in fact, how towers follow an oblique line coming down diagonally straight to the head of the Saint. Since the spatial content here is resolved in a systematic scaling down of cubical masses, this view of the city confronts us with an experience in terms of space which, though it may undoubtedly stem from an impression of reality, is ultimately as unnatural and, let it be said, as abstract or "metaphysical" as the apse and thrones of *The Vision*. Thus the city appears as if it were "summoned to the foreground by the firm and solemn gesture of man" (Mariani).

This vision of space, as a fact natural to the plastic substance of things, was similar to Arnolfo's. Giotto's acquaintance with the Florentine sculptor is confirmed by several details of form and theme repeatedly pointed out by critics, and we need not insist upon it here. It has been claimed, however, and rightly so, that among Giotto's decisive experiences before he began *The Legend of St Francis* was a study of Arnolfo's art and architecture. It is possible that, having completed the frescoes in the basilica's upper course, the master went to Rome to examine Arnolfo's canopies. He probably visited the Santa Reparata building site in Florence, where Arnolfo was directing the construction of the new cathedral and carving the figures for its façade while he was painting the *Crucifix* in the Church of Santa Maria Novella.

Nor is the principle differently applied in the more complicated compositions where the scenes are openly governed by an intuitive kind of perspective. In *The Miracle at Greccio* (plate 49), for instance, space, though ample and firm, is ultimately only a scale of volumes: the marble wall dividing the chapel from the body of the church is not a boundary but a solid volume and the canopy, so reminiscent of Arnolfo, the lectern, the pulpit and the crucifix tipped forward on the tripod into the church (plate 50) are all volumetric pieces, each one as enjoyable in itself as a still life. Their sole function is to qualify space as layers of volumes. Observe how the projection of the pulpit and crucifix beyond the marble wall into the main area of the church does not actually succeed in conveying the spatial idea of the nave, because all momentum is suddenly blocked by the hard chromatic plane of the background. Spatial content does not prevail over the plastic importance of each object. In *St Francis Preaching before Honorius III* (plate 60) the three great arches, which within their vaultings, contain the composition, repeat the treatment of space as it occurs below in the semi-circle of the three powerful figures. Again, in *The Apparition at Arles* (plate 62) the spacial content is entirely suggested by the transversal lay-out of the masses. Even Giotto's treatment of landscapes, much as their discovery moved him, never allows for wide horizons: any impression of reality emanating from them is not derived from a rich display of nature but, on the contrary, from the constriction of the spectacle within a solid architecture of volumes, such as the two trees in *St Francis Preaching to the Birds* (plate 56) or the two towering rocks in *The Miracle of the Spring* (plate 52).

What order, what wonderful simplicity in the composition of *St Francis Giving His Mantle to a Poor Knight* (plate 27)! Nature is more friendly here, and the artist's tender communion with it is made obvious by the little walled city and village church on the two hilltops and by the sprinkle of trees on the slopes. This picture, too, is nothing but a weaving together of equivalent volumes, in which even the triangle of sky between the two hillsides expresses not a void but an impenetrable mass. Far from being a diversion, the friendly participating aspect of nature in this fresco is an apt comment on the Franciscan *charitas* inspiring its central scene. Notice how each of the three figures—the two men and the horse—has a plastic continuity and development, from the surface on which they stand, behind them and upward into the sky. This continuity will be dominant in the Padua frescoes, as we shall see.

From such works sprung the myth of Giotto's "primitiveness," but the compact and simple rhythm of his composition is not childish, the very simplicity of his actions is not primitive. It is in fact an extreme simplification relative to the thirteenth century's pictorial tradition and has its poetic reasons in the conscious reduction of all visible things to their purest and most elementary plastic values. True, Giotto's plasticity had a precedent in that clear perception of relief displayed by Cavallini and generally by the Roman school but, especially in the Assisi frescoes, he departed from Cavallini's softness of contours and stressed his own concision and harshness of relief. This would appear to us rather as a translation of Arnolfo's synthesis and as a transposition, to the new plane of pictorial volumetry, of Cimabue's own harshness and tension. After all Giotto's *chiaroscuro* may have a richness and density directly derived from Cavallini, but it still shows none of the Roman master's *sfumato* quality: it makes volumes stand out and gleam like bronze under a hard light, as is the case here with the face of the knight. This can only derive from Cimabue.

But Cimabue's influence upon Giotto was also revealed

by the sharpness of the latter's outlines. We are not referring to certain mannerisms in the line—residues of archaic culture—appearing here and there in the St Francis cycle for instance the pleats in the mantle in the fresco in which the Saint gives away his mantle and the disarranged sheet in *The Dream of the Palace and Arms* (plate 30), certainly painted by an assistant from the Cimabue-Roman School, whose members were active in Assisi at the time. We mean the constant and positive function entrusted to the line, as a contour, in controlling volumes and in suggesting dynamic contrasts between them. Observe, in *St Francis Giving His Mantle to a Poor Knight*, what dramatic power is infused in the tense, incisive line of the knight's back, how it leaps out again after a brief pause at the waist, how it expresses in full, in terms of pure pictorial language, the mixture of pride and humility felt by a poor man of noble birth. See, in *St Francis Renouncing the World* (plate 32), how the wrathful father is held back not so much by his steward's feeble grip as by the tense energy controlling his own arm, by the act of will expressed in his strong profile and in the folds of the robe clutched in his left hand. It is the line, in this composition, that contains the volumes of the two opposed groups and at the same time connects them with the background which, in its turn, is given added tension by the void in the middle. In *St Francis Preaching before Honorius III* (plate 60) the firm profiles of the Saint on the left and the Pope in the centre are directly connected on a plane by-passing the seated prelates and including the column: thus a tension is created which translates into visual terms the intense psychological relationship between the two protagonists. Correctly, some critics have drawn attention to the importance of mime in Giotto's art and especially in the St Francis cycle. Often the explanation of a scene is limited to the discovery of its most concise or appropriate gesture. We must remark at this point that the undeniable effectiveness of mime in Giotto is raised from the level of mere illustration to that of poetry when a gesture becomes one with the line in the context of the function described above. Take one of the master's most simple and openly plastic compositions, such as *St Francis Preaching to the Birds*. The uniform blue area of the background was painted only to set out more vividly the powerful volumes of the figures, the plasticity of which is elementary, hardly articulated.

The curve of the Saint's back is charged with emotional meaning in that it contrasts with the almost vertical axis of the sturdy disciple's body continued by the slim little tree behind him. This group is now set out in a direct visual relationship with the one on the right, the birds at the Saint's feet and the curved trunk of the great tree behind them, the volume of which is also controlled by a hard line of contours. The surprised gesture of the first figure is a preparation—in the rhythm of its tense lines against the plane—for the more open posture of the Saint. Each necessary element to the illustration of the story is thus translated in terms of the purest form, and the whole composition depends on the delicate yet decisive action of separating the figure of the Saint from that of his friar against the motionless background of nature. This immediate visual impression is the essence of the painting.

Exalting the plasticity of all things was therefore Giotto's ultimate end in terms of style. But his volumes, seen at first in their elementary inarticulate absoluteness, break out of their isolation and establish a live relationship with one another through the sober though effective function of his contours. This, then, is the dynamic law of his compositions: the correlation of volumes by means of a plane. One could actually speak of a scale of tonalities going from the ancient bas-relief simplicity of scenes composed by setting a few figures against a single plane as in *St Francis Giving His Mantle to a Poor Knight*, *The Dream of Pope Innocent III* (plate 35), *The Vision of the Fiery Chariot*, *St Francis Preaching to the Birds* and *The Miracle of the Spring*, to those which include a large number of figures in groups either transversal or with a tendency to the semi-circular, such as *St Francis Preaching before Honorius III*, *The Sanctioning of the Rule* (plate 38) and *The Apparition at Arles*, which are all solemn works, impenetrably calm yet saturated with drama. Finally, there are the pictures in which the fulcrum of action is found in the convergence of two or more compositional main lines, ceremoniously grave at times, as in *The Miracle at Greccio*, at others drawn in a broken and hurried rhythm, as in the case of *The Death of the Knight of Celano* (plate 57) or of *The Lament of the Poor Clares* (plate 72).

The compositions in the first group prefigure the *Stories of the Virgin* in the Arena Chapel (see plates 98–107) and those in the second are a prelude to other Padua masterpieces such as *Christ Among the Elders* (plate 120), *The Last Supper* (plate 130) and *The Washing of the Feet* (plate 132). The last ones are precedents for more complex works such as *The Raising of Lazarus* (plate 124) and *The Lamentation* (plate 143). But in *The Legend of St Francis* composition, colors and relief are all typified by a violence of conquest—in the field of style—which is toned down somewhat in the works at Padua and those following. However, in *The Death of the Knight of Celano*, as in the Padua frescoes, we find an absolute organization of composition, the lines of which become more and more tense as they move from the inert little friar on the left—still sitting at table with his knife in the air—to the Saint's figure, spiritually so removed from the friar by the marked contours, to the greater tension of the group at the right and finally to the knight's dead body, where all tension ends. This passage, on the other hand, does not take place without interruptions and resumptions, such as the cloaked figure who seems to steer the Saint frontwards and the arched backs of the two women forming a lunette around the knight. Giotto, therefore, in this and other Assisi works, was searching for an intermittent rhythm.

This happens, too, in the beautiful *Lament of the Poor Clares*, the main lines of which were certainly by Giotto even if the actual execution was the work of pupils. Color as well, in Assisi, is more contrasting and discontinuous. The whole suggests a feeling of unforeseen and surprised revelation. Let us say that the hidden lyrical nucleus of *The Legend of St Francis* is the astonished contemplation of creation and a sense of wonder in the face of its miracle. One may even, though discreetly, suggest an affinity between Giotto's poetry and that of the Saint's *Fioretti* (short poems), but the artist's tone is more choral and solemn, for it contains the fore-knowledge of that supreme "necessity of events" which was to become his law at Padua.

In 1300 Giotto returned to Rome where he painted, in the Lateran Basilica, *Boniface VIII Proclaiming the Jubilee* (plate 78). The recently recovered fragments of this fresco show that he was greatly helped by his pupils: only the portrait of Cardinal Caetani (plate 79) may be considered an autograph. Those fragments, on the other hand, also provide unquestionable proof that Giotto painted *The Legend of St Francis* and that he did so in the last years of the thirteenth century. The *Navicella* mosaic instead (see Lost Paintings, page 85), traditionally accepted as a work of that period, is now thought to have been executed about ten years later.

The pictorial evidence of Giotto's subsequent activities in

Florence—the *Virgin and Child Enthroned* in San Giorgio alla Costa (plate 80) and *The Badia Polyptych* (plate 82)—though badly preserved, show a process of amplification of form and a deeper and calmer plasticity, clearly preparing the way for the Padua masterpieces. Only very recently were found and detached some fragments of a fresco in the Badia Church—where Ghiberti recalled a "chapel" as well as a "panel"—in which one may observe a style still rich with the power of expression that was present in Assisi but already broader and more inclusive.

Perhaps Giotto went for the first time to Rimini between his period of work in Rome and Florence. It is more certain that, presumably between 1304 and 1305, he painted the main part, and later *The Last Judgment* and the *Allegories* of the Arena Chapel in Padua. This is his greatest masterpiece (see plates 86–178). It could be that his renewed contacts with Roman circles induced him to study Pietro Cavallini's works from which he derived, partly at least, that greater blending of color and *chiaroscuro* which, in the Padua frescoes, appears to eliminate certain contrasts and breaks in continuity still visible in his Assisi paintings. But it could also be—and indeed it seems more probable—that this was a natural evolution taking place within the master's own personality. This argument is strengthened by the consideration that the firm and absolute light—a light without opposite—dominating and giving unity to the various stonelike tonalities of the Padua frescoes bears no relationship whatsoever to Cavallini's denser chromatism.

In Padua, Giotto's insistence upon incisiveness of outline, which was necessary in Assisi to contain the movement of his masses and to strengthen his dramatic mime was no longer necessary, each tension was resolved in itself by a constant modulation of masses closely connected with a plane. His forms became either softly rounded or clearly cut against flat planes; they were no longer drawn out from the background because of violent lights, as in Assisi. His dramatic feeling was now perhaps stronger than ever, but the spirit in which he expressed it was more serene. His masses became broader without prejudice to their effectiveness; his compositions more complex but also more compact, more closely concatenated in a slower rhythm.

Undoubtedly Giotto began working on the Chapel's upper walls, where he painted the *Stories of SS Joachim and Anne and the Virgin*, or the "pre-history" of Christ. He brought to this series a strange absorption, a slow but inflexible continuity of action, controlled by a quiet assurance which transformed his stories into the realization of a destiny traced by God. God, however, is identified with the moral conscience of Giotto's figures, who far from being manipulated from outside show an inner conviction and are capable of suffering their own drama to the last. This sense of fatality is stressed by a compositional concept based upon continuity of relief much as in a plastic frieze. The volumes are kept in direct and constant touch with an unbroken background which remains unchanged whether it portrays a rocky mountainside, as in the three scenes of Joachim's exile (plates 88, 92 and 94), or whether it is merely indicated by the continuous void behind the plane of the figures, as in *The Annunciation to St Anne* (plate 90), where the scene takes place in the supernatural silence of that square room in which the white curtain has the function of isolating from the figures in mid-distance the void behind them. In the two separate paintings of the *Annunciation* on either side of the triumphal arch (plate 106) in which, in spite of the figures' advanced position in their protruding niches, the room in which the vent takes place has no concrete image of space;

it is an emptiness which does not surround, a zone of stellar silence behind the absorbed figures. In the scant space before them, on the other hand, a play of tensions and distensions of volumes causes the forms to pulsate, and envelop the dramatic plot of the story in a slow and continuous harmony.

Let us pause, briefly, over each painting of this prehistory of Christ, and we shall immediately see how Giotto's new order of representational values which we have tried to describe, became ultimately a most sublime and expressive pictorial language, a poetry as limpid as spring water and yet charged—as much as Dante's—with moral significance. In *The Expulsion of Joachim from the Temple* (plate 86) the drama becomes immediate by the slow, inexorable rhythm of volumes proceeding towards the right, but this movement is suddenly arrested by the rotating figure of the Saint who has stopped on the edge of the platform, facing an empty surface of dense blue. This device makes the tension of the scene most durable. Let us now turn to *Joachim Retires to the Sheepfold* (plate 88). The continuity of the rock's face stresses the isolation of each figure and the concealed relationship between the smoother slope on the left and the towering, rugged stone above the shepherd's hut has an undefinable modulation of its own, both of *chiaroscuro* and outline, similar to a slow melodic accompaniment. Against this background we note the contrast between the figure of Joachim, enclosed in his robe and bending his head, and the square masses of the shepherds, who seem to be carved out of the rock itself: mute, sullen nature confronted by age and humanity. Look at *The Annunciation to St Anne* (plate 90) in which that much admired "still life," the chambermaid (plate 91), emerges, like Anne, from a space where the perspective is rigorously defined. Every object, however, is apparently deprived of its physical weight; even the flowers tossed by the angel seem fixed—rather than suspended—in mid-air, in a magic void where the law of gravity does not exist. After this rarefaction of human warmth we return to solitude, touched inevitably by sorrow, as we gaze upon the scenes of *Joachim's Dream* (plate 94) and of his *Sacrifice* (plate 92). The central gap in the skyline of the first picture, between the angel and the rock on the right, is matched by the rising altar in the *Sacrifice*, an incline for which we are prepared by the figure of the prostrated Saint. This liaison of masses and rhythms, based upon a play of balances, reappears in *The Meeting at the Golden Gate* (plate 96) where the tensions and distensions, almost a pulsation of forms, impart to the story a sense of depth and of detachment. Nothing is more solid than the towering gate, nothing more solemn than the ample archway. But the lively and colorful procession of women is blocked by the dark mass of the veiled woman (plate 97). This is a tonal solution worthy of Manet. The ideal axis of the composition is moved away from the geometrical one, towards the left tower, by the perfect ogee in which the two Saints embrace each other. Further on, after the first two *Stories of the Virgin*, we have the three scenes of the *Marriage* (plates 102–104); all are connected by the mysterious cross-section of the church and based on a slow, horizontal movement of masses suggesting the inevitability of fate. In the central picture, *The Prayer for the Blossoming of the Rods* (plate 103), the surface of blue coming down upon the heads of the kneeling crowd is similar to a held note in song and adds suspense and trepidation to the scene.

In the middle tier we find the first episode in the *Life of Christ* (*The Nativity* and *The Adoration of the Magi* [plates 110–111]). These resume, with a concatenation, the bas-relief composition; there is a uniformity of matter between rocky landscapes and figures stressing, as in the case of *Joachim Retires to the Sheepfold*, the continuity of the composition. From this a feeling of chaste simplicity is born, even though Giotto enriched with new elements the iconography of the thirteenth century. *The Flight into Egypt* (plate 116), too, recalls the *Stories of Joachim*, even in the size of its figures. The movement begun with the figures on the left is suddenly interrupted by the mountain rising beyond the Virgin. Then, with the descending slope, we come down to the figure of Joseph. Thus, by alternating motion with immobility, Giotto creates the visual impression of the journey's duration and fatal necessity.

But when we come to *The Massacre of the Innocents* (plate 118) and to *The Marriage at Cana* (plate 122) we detect, next to the horizontal movement, some new transversal directions and the rhythmical responses of volumes become more pregnant and complex. The composition gains in movement and in dramatic tempo until in *The Raising of Lazarus* (plate 124) we find the signs of that unresolved tension which always reappears during moments of great dramatic emotion: here the convergence upon Christ of the mountain-slope and of the women at his feet transfers most effectively the picture's focal point towards the side, while the lesser compositional high-light centered upon the swaddled Lazarus appears as a counterpart suggesting a greater orchestration. Still further, in *The Kiss of Judas* (plate 134) the drama has more than a mere choral comment, as it is enacted by the dark mass of figures in the background with the swinging torches projected towards the sky, while the excited figures in the foreground create an unbroken tension in what appears to be a single plastic mass. The very same plastic concept is manifest in *The Washing of the Feet* (plate 132), in which the slow rotation of volumes creates space through the energetic passages and rhythmical links. In other scenes, though, such as *Christ before Caiaphas* and *The Flagellation* (plates 136 and 138), the effects become complicated because of the significant breaks in composition. The figure of the Moor, whose surprising tone once again recalls Manet (the *Olympia* especially), separates the two groups. But the strict relationship of the gestures throughout the composition creates a dialectic with the interruption caused by the Moor, and the plane thus becomes more complex. These compositions are marked furthermore, by a certain sensual pleasure in the splendid details and in the unusual richness of modulations and *impasto*. This richness is a sign that these frescoes (we are speaking now of the lowest tier) were done after, and not before, the more sober "pre-history" in the upper tier.

But in these scenes from the Passion, the subject of which might have justifiably caused the artist to give in to a less controlled pathos, drama is still controlled by a firmness which in fact adds to its depth. For this reason we are not surprised by the quiet amosphere of *The Crucifixion* (plate 141) in which, however, the angel's full-throated lament in the sky tends to expand beyond all reasonable proportions if compared to the compact little group in the lower area around the crucified Redeemer. Here too, the picture's dramatic significance is expressed in terms of cosmic greatness. And where in fact we meet a cosmic tragedy, in which all life is stilled by universal sorrow, is in the very famous fresco of *The Lamentation* (plate 143). An organizational concept of many lines converges upon one point with a play of rotating volumes. This concentration of lines, ultimately resolved by that endless ledge of rock, is frozen in a total identity of spaces and volumes, whereby all the images of a tangible world—men and nature—are reduced to forms of the most absolute and elementary plasticity.

After such tremendous tension the cycle comes to a more serene conclusion—at least so far as Giotto's personal contribution to it is concerned—in the *Noli me tangere* (plate 147). The composition is broad and continuously modulated by the blended plasticity of landscape and figures; the colors are lively and perfectly attuned. See how the rosy light permeating the scene blends with the white robes of Christ and the angels, and how this general tenderness is made to contrast with the lyrical gesture of Mary Magdalen feeling her way with her thin arms into a void which again is stressed by the solid mass of her body draped in a red cloak (plate 149).

The decorations of the chapel's triumphal arch are worthy of special comment (plate 153). Here Giotto employed all his knowledge of the possibilities of space. From the deep but dilated space of the *Prologue in Heaven* (*Gabriel's Mission*) (plate 106), we proceed to volumetric space, such as in the two niches of the *Annunciation* protruding at the base of the lunette (plate 106), then to a high-relief, as in *The Visitation* (plate 108) and *The Hiring of Judas* where the dramatic tension is expressed in terms of forms against a plane. Finally we have the exact spatial perspective of the two *coretti*, or secret chapels, which unite one with the reality of the Arena Chapel itself, in that their perspective derives from a single point of view at the center of the nave (see plate 153). Here, in this precise relationship between real and representational space, Giotto reaches the threshold of fifteenth-century technique. It would be wrong, however, to consider the two secret chapels as the device of a virtuoso or as an escape on Giotto's part, into a realm that is not quite his own. Let us see what their function is in the whole of the triumphal arch. They are, in fact, a necessary counterpart, in terms of perspective, to the two niches of the *Annunciation*, which not only protrude, but converge, whereas the interiors of the two chapels diverge towards separate points. The synthesis of these opposites is assured by the uppermost composition of the *Prologue in Heaven*, which seems to absorb both the protrusion of the niches and the cavities of the *coretti* into a metaphysical kind of space, obtained by scaling the volumes against the plane. The unearthly quality of this space is perfectly consonant with the atmosphere of solemn detachment governing the entire cycle about Christ in the Arena Chapel.

There is not enough room, here, to comment extensively upon the *Allegories of Vices and Virtues* (plates 166–171), painted in monochrome with a few touches of color in the lowest tier. They are mostly autograph. If their general tone is fundamentally prosaic, such coldness is amply compensated by the depth of psychology which Giotto attained, and by their moral quality. In fact, the vigor of his invention engenders, occasionally, real poetry as in the pictures of *Wrath* (plate 168), of *Hope* (plate 170), of *Charity* (plate 167) and of *Injustice* (plate 169). As far as *The Last Judgment* (plates 155–165) is concerned, this was painted, for the greater part, by Giotto's pupils, though we may admire, as suggested by Battisti, the imagery and harsh efficacy of some details of *Hell* (plates 164–165) and acknowledge, as all critics do, the beauty of the *Virgin*, of the *Eternal Father* and of the group of the *Dedication* (plate 161) which are among the few autograph parts by Giotto. We shall be forced, however, to conclude, with Gnudi, that "In Giotto's poetry what is transcendent always dominates reality and all representation of reality is constantly referred to this relationship, to an ideal and necessary presence; but the tangible representation of a super-world, of the infinite, of God, remains a description or a symbol; it is never translated into another, or a different poetic reality."

Some time after the Padua masterpiece Giotto was to paint the great *Madonna and Child in Glory* for the Church of Ognissanti in Florence, now in the Uffizi Gallery (plates 185–189). The panel shares with the Padua frescoes some thick outlines, blended in *chiaroscuro*, so different from the dry clear-cut contours of the Assisi paintings. The Virgin, especially so in the lower part of her body, is as powerful as the women seen from the back in *The Lamentation*, but her figure fills the throne completely, leaving no hiatus whatsoever. The throne itself, with its gables and protruding steps, absorbs all the space in the picture, while the angels on either side of the aedicule seem to mark, with their haloes, the series of plastic planes making up the composition. Not even the six angels in the extreme background are outside the spatial area claimed by the throne; in fact, they strengthen and proclaim afresh the composition's plastic unity, turning it into a solid block inside which a consistent and silent relationship takes place between the worshippers and the adored, as punctuated by the fixity of each figure's eyes. This supreme, but still tightly constructed balance marks the transition from the Padua style to that of the *Stories of St Francis* in Santa Croce.

A document of December 1313 shows that Giotto had returned to Rome a few years before, in all probability to execute there the *Navicella* mosaic. That this followed the Padua frescoes appears to be convincingly indicated by the solemn, open composition and by the two remaining *Angels* (plate 179) with their rich, graduated colors. A few years later the master was once again in Padua, and worked there (ancient records mention the *Astrological Frescoes* in the

Comune's Palace Hall, but these have been lost). Perhaps this was when Giotto painted the *Crucifix* (plate 182) in the Arena Chapel and another in the Tempio Malatestiano in Rimini (plate 180) which repeats the iconographical scheme but, as aptly observed by E. Battisti, "with a new effective quality which gives it a matchless lyrical intensity."

Quite some time later Giotto decorated the Peruzzi Chapel in the Church of Santa Croce in Florence with frescoes of the *Stories of the Two St Johns* (plates 190–195), and later still the Bardi Chapel in the same church with the *Stories of St Francis* (plates 196–217). All these frescoes, but especially the former, are in very poor condition because of early restorations. One can still appreciate, however, the value of their composition and plastic rhythm. Both cycles depart from the Padua frescoes in that their composition is less compact, their rhythm more relaxed, their tempo slower. The Peruzzi frescoes, however, show a greater complexity of forms, and a greater agility of movement and richness of invention, at times even a heroic emphasis, far removed from the supernatural quiet of the paintings in the Bardi Chapel. In *The Ascension of St John the Evangelist* (plate 195) the balanced composition is suddenly liberated, as it were, by the precipitous opening in the edifice through which the Saint rises, leaving an empty space beneath him, and the bystanders are divided and pushed back towards the sides as if by an uncanny eruption. This realization of the forceful composition we came to know in Padua toward a more monumental organization can be found again, though with a different stress, in *The Raising of Drusiana* (plate 194). Here the two choral groups confronting each other are compact, but relaxed, and their monumentality is matched by the buildings behind them. The wall, turning in at the center, creates a dynamic void, as in *The Ascension*. Furthermore, the pattern of that architecture now jutting forward, now falling back, has not so much the function of emphasizing the illusion of space, but rather of creating a constant rebound of forces, in order to multiply and reinforce the tension of the planes.

In *The Dance of Salome* (plate 192), which was perhaps the last fresco painted by Giotto in the Peruzzi Chapel, we find a sedate, broadened balance, far removed from earlier tensions, and possibly even more obvious at the time of execution, before the disappearance of John's head looking out from the prison's window at the left, as evidenced from the study of fourteenth-century replicas. But even though Giotto's rhythms are slower here, his typical plastic continuity remains unchanged. The whole picture is substantially based upon two parallel planes of development connected by the key volume of the musician's figure, echoed by the massive tower behind him.

What Giotto's expression, in its almost pure state, was at the time of the Peruzzi Chapel can be seen in *The Death of the Virgin* in Berlin (plate 218), originally in the Church of Ognissanti, Florence. This work, which appears to have been painted mainly by Giotto alone, is an imposing and yet not trying composition, though not entirely devoid of a sense of poise and of sculptural attitudes. The same cannot be said, in our view, of the series of small panels with the *Life of Christ*, now distributed among galleries in New York, Boston, London, Florence and Munich (plates 238–244), in which the power of execution falls short of the beauty of composition and general rhythm. True, *The Adoration of the Magi* (plate 238) has an intimate atmosphere, due to its bas-relief composition, and the horizontal rhythm of *The Presentation of Christ in the Temple* (plate 239), set against the void created by the perspective pavement and canopy, is fascinating. Space is made to look hard and clear in *The Pentecost* (plate 244) while the figures of *The Deposition* (plate 242) are softly modulated under the low skyline with hills. One can hardly believe that these scenes were conceived by a pupil, though assistants might have been responsible for less original compositions, such as the three Munich compartments (plates 240–241 and 243). But even in the best of these works the figures seem to be too short of weight necessary to sustain the intensity of rhythm of the compositions, which however surely reflected some of Giotto's thoughts in the period between his work in the Bardi and Peruzzi Chapels.

In the Bardi Chapel all tension is stilled in an absolute vision of order and sublime serenity, even where Giotto summons back a theme or two from the Assisi cycle. This newly found, slow-paced rhythm led some critics to assume, with reason, that the artist had become by now thoroughly acquainted with the works of Ambrogio Lorenzetti, who was active in the Florentine countryside before 1320. It could be that Lorenzetti and Giotto influenced one another, but too little is known about the painter from Siena in his early days to state categorically if and to what extent he contributed to this, the master's finest phase. What we do know is that such a development was logical and even foreseeable, because of the direction taken by Giotto's art after the Padua frescoes.

The excellent restoration work recently carried out upon the Bardi frescoes has shown that, with the exception of the two lunettes of *St Francis Renouncing the World* (plate 196) and *The Sanctioning of the Rule* (plate 198), in which the assistants' work is decidedly obvious, those solemn masterpieces were largely devised and painted by Giotto alone. All the main scenes take place inside well defined frontal areas, so that space itself, clearly conceived in terms of depth, finds

34

a peaceful and constant relationship with the plane, in a perfect fusion such as once before, in the last works at the Arena Chapel, had produced magnificent results. Throughout, beginning with the scene of *The Apparitions to the Bishop and to Friar Augustine* (plate 212), a sublime harmony embraces the vast horizontal rhythm of the simple, clear, spatial structure and the slower one of the volumes throbbing along the plane, while their regression in depth achieves the effect of a counterpoint. Volume and space are no longer two opposed dialectical terms but almost the double aspect of a single reality, two mysterious allies in an easy flowing—though still solemn—rhythm of composition, favored by warm and dense colors which seem to have captured and appropriated the quality of *chiaroscuro*. *The Ordeal by Fire* (plate 200) is one of the most intense compositions from the chromatic point of view. In characterizing the scene's noble décor, the white robes of the servants, the rich and colorful ones of the Sultan and his dignitaries, the dark complexions of the Moors, color operates inside light as a spirit of truth (with complete regard to its own laws), as it follows a slow, sedate modulation in perfect harmony with the relaxed motions of the participants. A severe, musical order controls the Sultan's gesture and the withdrawal of the shamed-faced Moorish priests. This is what, in depriving the scene of all sensational immediacy, confers upon it a majestic and almost sacred character. The dramatic content is not lost but enhanced with ritual composure to a level of higher and more essential truth. These are the aspects of Giotto's art which were to be retained and developed more substantially not many years later by Masaccio, in another chapel in Santa Croce.

In *The Apparition at Arles* (plate 204) the scene is given a new width by the three arches, but space exists, however, merely functioning as a connective tissue of the volumes. Giotto achieves here a particularly unifying plasticity by alternating the brown cowls of the spiritual and black ones of the conventual monks into a perfect texture of volumes exalted by the central high note of the Saint's figure in the middle arch. A mysterious suggestion of eternity dominates this and other frescoes, especially that of *The Death of St Francis* (plate 208), in which the various groups are either slowly approaching or facing the Saint's body and the tempo of their movements is regularly scanned by the partitions in the background. Here, too, space and rhythm of volumes are blended in an absolute plastic homogeneity. The Saint's soul, high in the sky, marks the central axis of the composition, but the convergence of the groups of monks creates a new ideal center around the head of Francis. This induces, in the midst of such peace, a subtle element of tension, enough to allow, in pure representational terms, for the emotional content of the scene—in other words, for the community's tender sorrow. The composition's extreme concision of style is reflected in its details, such as the geometric essentiality of the friars' tonsures or some of the faces, which never interfere in the slightest with the unity of the whole. Such a capacity for a reconstruction of reality calls Cézanne to mind, but in the blending of the various elements there is also a softness of form and color, mitigating the solemn character of the whole picture.

Now that the Bardi frescoes have been rendered very similar to the original product of Giotto's brush, even in the coloring, one should feel more confident about attributing to the master the Kress *Madonna* in Washington (plate 223), the *St Stephen* in the Horne Museum in Florence (plate 222) and the *SS John the Evangelist and Lawrence* in Châalis (plates 224–225). This last work is plastically so modulated and the substance of its color is such that it can compare most favorably with the Bardi frescoes, even though the figure of St John the Evangelist is more reminiscent of the humanity in the Peruzzi frescoes. Here, too, we enjoy a serene vision, sweet and rich with lyrical depth. The preciousness of the ornaments upon St Stephen's dalmatic robe is more than a mere embellishment, for it becomes entirely integrated into the general modulation of form without, as Ghiberti would have put it, "exceeding the boundaries."

From 1329 to 1333 Giotto worked in Naples, where he had been called by Robert of Anjou, to whom he had probably been recommended by the Bardi family who were, among other things, the bankers of the King of Naples. He had with him Maso to whom one could attribute (Salmi) some of the remaining parts of the frescoes in the Chapel at Castelnuovo. In 1334 he was appointed by the Florence Republic, "Master of the works of the Cathedral and architect of the city walls and fortifications." On July 19 he laid the foundation stone of the Campanile which, though continued by others, still preserves his name and the mark of his style. Between 1335 and 1336 he went to Milan where he painted, in the palace of Azzo Visconti, a *Vana Gloria* (*Worldly Glory*) surrounded by the "most illustrious ancient princes of the world."

But all that has disappeared. Some works bearing his name, or rather the trademark of his workshop, such as the *Coronation* polyptych in the Baroncelli Chapel in Santa Croce (plate 247) and the altarpiece of the *Virgin and Saints* formerly in Santa Maria degli Angeli in Bologna and now in the Pinacoteca there (plate 246), are mainly the work of his students. What little belongs to the master reflects the style of the Bardi Chapel. In the same period, or perhaps during Giotto's visit to Naples, a triptych was produced for

Cardinal Stefaneschi in St Peter's and can now be seen in the Vatican Pinacoteca (plate 250), but it was all executed by followers. To this last period belong also the *Crucifixions* of Berlin and Strasbourg (plates 254–255) which, with a few other works, some would attempt nowadays to include in the master's *corpus*, but they are obviously the product of his school or workshop and can tell us nothing more—assuming that they may be considered as evidence of his final development—than what we have learned directly from the frescoes of the two chapels in Santa Croce.

Giotto died in Florence on January 8, 1337, aged seventy. During his life he achieved great fame as recorded by Dante, and Petrarch. Boccaccio's recounting of his fame leaves no doubt that his contemporaries fully acknowledged that, with him, a new representational language had been born.

Giotto indeed, as Cennino Cennini wrote shortly before 1400, "translated that art of painting from Greek into Latin, and made it modern." Today the attention focused by critics upon his accomplishments in terms of space, his discovery of the perspective law of convergence toward a single vanishing point, which he applied at least in the two *coretti* at Padua, establishes him as a greater master than Ambrogio Lorenzetti in the field of perspective and strengthens the argument of those who would see in him, rather than in Masaccio, the pioneer of the Renaissance. We have seen, on the other hand, how his capacity for achieving a vision of space which is perfectly credible was brought to bear by Giotto only in exceptional cases, for such a vision of space was not consistent with the canons of his world, in which Man's actions are still governed by a moral law and by an absolute order which transcends him. We have seen how even those brief excursions of Giotto in the realms of nature were merely dialectical, inserted in a totally different organism. His vision was not, therefore, Masaccio's vision and the principle of nature as a separate reality and of man's independence from it had yet to be discovered.

It is also true, however, that his supreme clarity of expression, his magnificent synthesis, the assurance of his plastic compositions, make of Giotto, if not one of the inventors, certainly the prophet of the Renaissance and one of the founders of a language spoken for centuries (until recently) by our painters.

BIOGRAPHICAL NOTES

1267(?). Giotto di Bondone is born at Colle, near Vespignano, a few miles north of Florence. His father, Vasari writes, "tilled the soil and was a humble person." The date of birth is testified by Antonio Pucci who, in 1373, wrote that Giotto had died in 1337 (1336 by the Florentine Calendar), aged seventy. Vasari, however, claims that he was born in 1276 and some have thought that Pucci's statement was due to his having confused the Italian *sessanta* (sixty) with *settanta* (seventy). It is now proved that Giotto was born, as claimed by Vasari, in Colle di Vespignano and not, as stated by Del Badia, in Florence.

1285–90. During this period he is thought to have been apprenticed to Cimabue at Florence and to have traveled for the first time to Rome.

1291–95. First worked in the Upper Church of San Francesco in Assisi (*Stories of Isaac, Stories of Joseph and from the New Testament*) on the uppermost tier of the walls, in the first two bays near the entrance.

1297–99. Paints the *Legend of St Francis* in San Francesco.

1300. Is in Rome, where he paints *Boniface the VIII Proclaiming the Jubilee of 1300* in the Basilica of St John Lateran. It is doubtful that at this time he also executed the *Navicella* mosaic in St Peter's.

1301. Two documents of May 25 and 26 concerning the sale of a house *in burgo de foris a Porta Panzani* at Florence state that it borders the property of Giotto of Bondone.

1304–6. Frescoes in the Arena Chapel of the Scrovegni family in Padua.

1305. A document of November of that year states that Giotto owned a house, leased to a saddler, in Florence, in the quarter of San Pancrazio, Parish of Santa Maria Novella.

1311–12. Documents prove that the master is in Florence where, among other things, he hires out a loom (*telarium francigenum*) to Bartolo di Rinuccio.

1313. Giotto is in Florence, trying to recover certain household articles belonging to him from his Roman landlady; one draws from this the conclusion that he was in that city before 1313, possibly in 1310.

1314. Documents prove that Giotto is in Florence.

1315, OCTOBER. Fights a legal battle with Grimaldo, a notary, for the ownership of a piece of land at Colle di Vespignano.

1318. He enfranchises his son Francesco—*qui hodie moratur Vespignani*—in order to donate through him a piece of land near San Michele di Aglioni to his daughter Bice.

1320. Documents prove that Giotto is in Florence.

1320–25(?). In this period Giotto is thought to have painted the frescoes in the Peruzzi and Bardi Chapels in Santa Croce.

1325, AUGUST. He makes the final payment to Bettino di Pace for lands purchased from him in Colle di Vespignano.

1326. Marriage contract for his second daughter Chiara made on February 17. Grants her a dowry on May 12.

1327. Enrolls in the guild of Physicians and Apothecaries, to which artists had only recently been admitted.

1329. Francesco, son of Giotto, acting on his father's behalf, hires out a piece of land in San Michele di Aglioni.

1329–33. Various documents testify to Giotto's presence in Naples, where he works at the court of Robert of Anjou. He is admitted to the circle of the King's intimate friends.

1331. Francesco sells a small farm at Pesciolo on behalf of his father.

1334. Francesco, as his father's agent, rents a piece of land at San Michele di Aglioni.

1334, APRIL 12. Giotto is appointed by the Florentine Republic master of the works of the Cathedral and architect of the city walls and fortifications. On July 19, as stated by Villani, the foundation stone of the Campanile is laid.

1335–36. Giotto is in Milan, working for Azzone Visconti (Villani).

1337, JANUARY 8. Giotto dies in Florence (Villani). In a document of July 4 Monna Ciuta is named as his widow.

GIOTTO'S PAINTINGS

THE ASSISI FRESCOES

BIBLICAL STORIES

(Plates 1–19 and 230–233)

The series of frescoes with stories from the Old and New Testaments decorating the higher part of the two walls of the nave (in compartments roughly 3 meters wide) and the entrance wall (in compartments roughly 3 × 4 meters) of the Upper Church of San Francesco in Assisi is the work of several artists, who were probably of the Roman school, and not clearly identified. (See the sketch on the next page; the numbers correspond to those of our plates.)

One of the main problems in this connection is the chronological one of distinguishing Cimabue's work in Assisi from Giotto's early works. We assume, for many reasons, that the former worked on the choir and transept walls between 1277 and 1280 (the era of Pope Nicholas III, whose family crest appears three times on the ceiling fresco) and that Giotto began to paint the *Legend of St Francis* in 1296 or 1297 after executing, possibly between 1291 and 1295, the frescoes of the *Stories of Isaac*, the *Stories of Joseph* and some of the scenes from the New Testament. These chronological theories, as well as Giotto's authorship of the *Legend* and other paintings, have been bitterly disputed. As far as the *Legend* is concerned see the next chapter.

With regard to the Biblical and New Testament scenes it is our contention that in *The Lamentation* (plate 11) many general and detailed elements bring to mind similar works by Giotto at Assisi and Padua, and the figures recall the two mourners in the horizontal arm of the *Crucifix* in Santa Maria Novella at Florence (plates 22–23). If, furthermore, one assigns to the master the *Lament* and the *Resurrection*, then one should accept his authorship of all the other frescoes under the fourth vaulting (*Baptism of Christ, Christ among the Elders* above and, on the opposite wall, *Stories of Cain and Abel* and *Stories of Joseph*). Contrary to our previously published statements, we are now convinced that the *Stories of Isaac* are also by Giotto. Our argument was that the concept of space in those frescoes was so different from that of *The Legend of St Francis* as to make any *rapprochement* impossible. We must acknowledge now, in the face of the many clear affinities of physiognomy and mime between the figures in the two cycles that the diversity of spatial conception, real though it is, is not irreconcilable. (See Life and Work, pages 11–13.)

Plate 1

ISAAC BLESSING JACOB. (See also plate 2.)

Plate 2
ISAAC BLESSING JACOB. Detail:
Jacob's head.

Plate 3
ISAAC REJECTING ESAU. (See also
plates 4–5.)

Plate 4
ISAAC REJECTING ESAU. Detail:
Isaac's bust.

Plate 5
ISAAC REJECTING ESAU. Detail:
young woman.

Plate 6
THE BAPTISM OF CHRIST. (See
also plate 7.)

Plate 7
THE BAPTISM OF CHRIST. Detail:
busts of two bystanders.

Plate 8
CHRIST AMONG THE ELDERS.
(See also plate 9.)

Plate 9
CHRIST AMONG THE ELDERS. Detail: bust of Jesus.

Plate 10
THE SLAYING OF ABEL.

Plate 11
THE LAMENTATION. (See also
plates 12–14.)

Plate 12
THE LAMENTATION. Detail: St
John's head.

Plate 13
THE LAMENTATION. Detail: Virgin's head.

Plate 14
THE LAMENTATION. Detail: busts
of two mourning women.

Plate 15
THE RESURRECTION.

Plate 16
JOSEPH IS SOLD BY HIS BRETH-
REN. (See also plate 17.)

Plate 17
JOSEPH IS SOLD BY HIS BRETH-
REN. Detail: Joseph's brothers.

Plate 18
THE FINDING OF THE CUP IN
BENJAMIN'S SACK. (See also plate
19.)

Plate 19
THE FINDING OF THE CUP IN
BENJAMIN'S SACK. Detail: Joseph's
brothers.

Plate 20
CRUCIFIX. *Panel, 578 × 406.** Florence, Santa Maria Novella.* Ghiberti
is among the earliest sources which
mention Giotto's *Crucifix.* In 1312
Riccuccio, son of the late Puccio del
Mugnaio, left in his will a sum of
money for a lamp to be kept burning
by the *Crucifix* in Santa Maria
Novella, painted by Giotto.

Doubts may, of course, arise as to
whether this particular work—
which remained on the church's
entrance wall from 1530 until the
last war, as proved by Antonio Billi
in his *Libro*—is the same as the one
mentioned in Riccuccio's will. In
fact, critics opposed the attribution
for a long time. But just before the
Giotto Exhibition of 1937, when the
Crucifix was cleaned and closely
examined, the majority of scholars
(Coletti, Salmi, Oertel, Toesca,
Longhi) voted in favor of Giotto.
The theory is not accepted, however,
by those who would reject totally
all of Giotto's early works (Perkins,

* All dimensions are given in centimeters.

Offner; see following comment on *The Legend of St Francis* at Assisi), and by Brandi, for reasons of style and because Crowe and Cavalcaselle, in their 1875 edition, state that the *Crucifix* had been transferred only a short time previously to the church's wall from a chapel. This information, however, remains an isolated fact, and in the face of the other critics' unanimity one can only assume that Crowe and Cavalcaselle were wrong.

More recently, while Offner (*Corpus*, III, Vol. VI, 1956) assigns it to a "Master of the Cross in Santa Maria Novella," together with the *Madonna of San Giorgio alla Costa* (plate 80), Brandi has modified his stand on this *Crucifix* and now admits that it could be attributed to Giotto in about 1300, though he ascribes the two doleful half-length figures, one at each extremity of the arms of the Cross, to the artist who painted *The Lamentation* and other frescoes at Assisi, which Brandi assigns to an older man than Giotto, but certainly influenced by him.

In our view the style of the *Crucifix* is fully consistent with Giotto's early stages between *The Lamentation* and *The Legend of St Francis*, therefore about 1295–96. (Longhi, Gnudi, and Battisti, on the other hand, favor the date 1290, while Meiss considers it the work of a distinguished pupil executed shortly before 1300.)

In the fresco, *The Testing of the Stigmata* (plates 69–71), a crucifix appears (top center) very similar to this one and the lateral figures of the mourners closely resemble those of *The Lamentation*. Also worthy of note are the remarks by W. Schone (in *Festschrift Friedrich Winkler*, 1959) about the importance of this work in the evolution from the "painted cross" of the thirteenth century to the "Crucifix" understood as a "picture" in the modern sense. (See also plates 21–23.)

Plate 21
CRUCIFIX. Detail: Christ's head.

Plate 22
CRUCIFIX. Detail: the Virgin.

Plate 23
CRUCIFIX. Detail: St John.

THE LEGEND OF ST FRANCIS

(Plates 24–77)

The Legend is told in twenty-eight frescoes framed by painted ledges and columns upon the lower course of the walls of the nave and of the entrance wall on the two sides of the portal (*Miracle of the Spring* and *St Francis Preaching to the Birds*, plates 52–56) in the Upper Church of San Francesco in Assisi. Over the portal, inside a fake architectural frame (see plan on page 44), there is a medallion with half-length figures of the *Virgin and Child* flanked by two smaller medallions with half-length figures of Angels. This cycle, traditionally attributed to Giotto but with little evidence, is still a subject of learned dispute. Vasari, in the second edition of his *Lives* (1568), is the first to attribute these works to Giotto, though he mistakenly writes about thirty-two stories. In 1450 Ghiberti had probably referred to these frescoes when he wrote that

Giotto "painted almost the whole of the lower part of the Assisi Church belonging to the *Frati Minori*." In fact, it is likely that he meant the lower part of the Upper Church rather than the Lower Church, where there is no fresco that one may attribute to Giotto. After Vasari, for two centuries and a half, the attribution was more or less undisputed until Witte in 1821 and Rumohr in 1827 opposed Giotto's authorship for reasons of style. A critical tide thus started, involving Rintelen in 1912, Offner in 1939 and recently Roy Fisher (*Art Bulletin*, 1956); the latter having established that Giotto's *The Lament of the Poor Clares* (plate 72), with its tree-climbing boy, was derived from *The Entry in Jerusalem* (plate 126) in Padua, then advances the date of the whole Assisi cycle, thereby disclaiming Giotto as its painter. In their conviction these critics do not stop for a moment to consider the development of the master's personality and insist that his first works were those in the Scrovegni Chapel in Padua, which are so mature.

This school of thought—joined by Meiss in 1960 and by A. Smart, in *Burlington Magazine*, 1960—base their contention upon the deep differences in style between the Assisi and the Padua frescoes, and especially upon the different conceptions of space governing the two cycles. The opposite, and in our opinion the right theory—which for reasons of space cannot be fully developed here—shall triumph when the whole of Giotto's *corpus* will have been submitted to a thorough critical reconstruction in which the spacial conceptions and pictorial languages of the Padua and Florence frescoes will be shown to be admittedly different, because they are, but not irreconcilable with those of the Assisi *Legend*.

The Italian critics have been making this comparison for some time, from Adolfo and Lionello Venturi to Luzzatto, Cecchi, Toesca, Brandi, Gnudi and others.

Other arguments, too, support the thesis of Giotto's authorship of the Assisi frescoes. First, the evidence of his contemporary Riccobaldo of Ferrara who, in about 1312, wrote that Giotto was working in the Franciscan Church in Assisi. This can only refer to the Upper Church paintings, for nothing, in the lower one, is by the master. It is highly improbable that a report written in Giotto's own time could be mistaken. Another argument is provided by the *Stigmata* panel in the Louvre. It is signed: *opus Jocti florentini*, but most scholars believe it the work of a very mediocre pupil. However, to give it authenticity, the painter reproduced in its predella three of the Assisi stories. (See Paintings Attributed to Giotto.) A further important argument is to be found in the Rimini school of the fourteenth century. The style of those artists, in its early stages, is clearly similar to that of *The Legend of St Francis*, and Riccobaldo states that Giotto worked for a time in the Franciscan Church at Rimini—though no record has been found of this activity. But, if Giotto was in Rimini, how could those painters have failed to succumb to his magic, and yet be influenced by the unknown master of the *Legend* in far away Assisi?

More recently (in *Burlington Magazine*, 1956) White observed that the Boston *St Francis Receiving the Stigmata* by Giuliano da Rimini, dated 1307, presupposes the *Stigmata* fresco in the *Legend* in Assisi.

For these and other reasons we believe the thesis that the *Legend* was the work of a late Giottesque who painted it about the middle of the fourteenth century to be no longer valid.

If one accepts Giotto's authorship of the Assisi cycle, then the date must perforce be shifted back. In the second edition of his *Lives* Vasari states that the master was asked to paint the *Legend* by Fra Giovanni di Muro della Marca, General of the Order, between 1296 and 1305. Murray (*Journal of the Warburg and Courtauld Institutes*, 1953) doubts the authenticity of the biographer's documentation, but he also takes issue against those who would bring forward the execution of the *Legend* to a good many years after 1300; in fact, he sees a connection between *The Dream of Pope Innocent III* (plate 35) and the reconstruction of the Lateran Portico under Nicholas IV, who reigned between 1291 and 1292.

1305, furthermore, must be considered a term *ante quem*, for in that year the *Tower of the People* was completed in Assisi, whereas we see it still unfinished in the cycle's first fresco. Everyone who allots the cycle to Giotto, at any rate believes that it was painted before the Padua frescoes (1305), in fact quite some time before, because of the differences in style. And as Giotto, in the Jubilee year, was working in Rome—if not on the *Navicella* mosaic, at least on the Lateran fresco (plate 78)—it is reasonable to argue that the Assisi cycle was completed, as far as Giotto was concerned, before 1300, perhaps in 1298. Two years may seem a short time, but he worked quickly and, let us not forget, was helped by many assistants who probably, as Gnudi assumes, continued the work from his drawings after the master had left Assisi.

That Giotto did not paint the frescoes alone is universally recognized. However, and this is the seal of a great artistic personality—no attempt to identify the various contributions has been successful with the exception of the last nine compartments following *St Francis Receiving the Stigmata* (plate 63), where Giotto's participation and even his design become rarefied to an extreme degree, except for *The Lament of the Poor Clares*, executed by more than one pupil but from Giotto's design. The last three compartments are almost unanimously attributed to the "Master of St Cecilia" whose *Scenes from the Life of St Cecilia* are in the Uffizi, and for that reason they are not reproduced in this book. The same artist has been considered— and rightly so—responsible for part at least of the fourth before the last fresco, *The Apparition to Gregory IX* (plate 76).

The measurements of the single frescoes are all about 270 (height) × 230 (width), with the exception of the two frescoes upon the entrance wall (plates 52 and 56), which are only about 200 wide.

Plate 24
MEDALLION WITH THE VIRGIN AND CHILD.

Plate 25
MEDALLIONS WITH ANGELS.

Plate 26
ST FRANCIS BEING HONORED BY A SIMPLE MAN. This and the following episodes illustrated in the cycle are derived from the text of the legend published by St Bonaventure between 1260 and 1263 and based upon the very first biographies of St Francis and oral tradition, which was still very much alive in Assisi.

Each fresco was explained by an inscription in Latin, which in most cases has gradually faded away. They were, however, reconstructed by Father Bonaventura Marinangeli, and we shall quote them as such. The one relating to this fresco reads: *Cum vir simplex de Assisio sternit vestes beato Francisco fuditque honores ipsi eunti, super hoc, creditur eruditus a Deo, asserens omni Franciscum reverentia dignum, quia esset in proximo magna facturus, ed ideo ab omnibus honorandus.* (How a simple man of Assisi laid down his cloak before the feet of the Blessed Francis as he was passing, and furthermore—inspired, it is believed, by God—stated that Francis was worthy of all reverence, for he was destined to do great things in the future, and therefore everyone should pay him honor.)

Plate 27

ST FRANCIS GIVING HIS MANTLE TO A POOR KNIGHT. "This is when the Blessed Francis met a noble but impoverished knight and was moved to compassion by his plight, so that he immediately disrobed and gave him his cloak." (See also plates 28–29.)

Plate 28

ST FRANCIS GIVING HIS MANTLE TO A POOR KNIGHT. Detail: landscape.

Plate 29

ST FRANCIS GIVING HIS MANTLE TO A POOR KNIGHT. Detail: the poor knight.

Plate 30

THE DREAM OF THE PALACE AND ARMS. "The following night, the Blessed Francis having fallen asleep, he saw a splendid palace, adorned with arms of war, bearing the symbol of the Savior's Cross; when he asked to whom they belonged a celestial voice answered that they would all belong to him and to his soldiers." While confirming that Francis had earlier been attracted to a military career, this is also an allegory of the Christian Militia that he was to found.

Plate 31

THE CRUCIFIX OF ST DAMIAN SPEAKS TO ST FRANCIS. "As the Blessed Francis prayed by the Crucifix, a voice from the Cross repeated three times: 'Francis, go, repair my home which is being destroyed,' alluding to the Church of Rome."

Plate 32

ST FRANCIS RENOUNCING THE WORLD. "How he returned all his goods to his father and, having removed his clothes, renounced his paternal and temporal goods, telling his father: 'From now on I may confidently say: Our Father who art in Heaven, for Pietro of Bernardone has repudiated me.'" (See also plates 33–34.)

Plate 33

ST FRANCIS RENOUNCING THE WORLD. Detail: the Bishop.

Plate 34

ST FRANCIS RENOUNCING THE WORLD. Detail: two children.

Plate 35

THE DREAM OF POPE INNOCENT III. "The Pope saw the Lateran Basilica about to fall in ruins, when a poor man, the Blessed Francis, put his shoulder underneath it and held the church up." (See also plates 36–37.)

Plate 36

THE DREAM OF POPE INNOCENT III. Detail: St Francis supporting the Lateran Basilica.

Plate 37

THE DREAM OF POPE INNOCENT III. Detail: the sleeping Pope.

Plate 38

THE SANCTIONING OF THE RULE. "How Pope Innocent III approved the Franciscan Rules and gave that order a mandate to preach penance, commanding the friars who were with the Saint to fashion Rosaries, so that they may preach the Word of God." (See also plate 39.)

Plate 39

THE SANCTIONING OF THE RULE. Detail: the Pope.

Plate 40

THE VISION OF THE FIERY CHARIOT. "As the Blessed Francis was at prayer in a hovel, and his friars in another hovel in the city, some resting and others persevering in prayer, and all far from him, after some time they saw the Blessed Francis mounted upon a fiery chariot rushing about their hovel close upon midnight, while the hut became resplendent with light; whereupon those who were awake marveled and those who were sleeping awoke and were afraid." (See also plate 41.)

Plate 41

THE VISION OF THE FIERY CHARIOT. Detail: sleeping friar.

Plate 42

THE VISION OF THE THRONES. "How the celestial vision appearing to a friar showed him many thrones in the sky, and one throne nobler than the others, and the friar heard a voice saying: 'This throne belonged to one of the fallen angels, and is now bespoken for humble Francis.'" (See also plate 43.)

Plate 43

THE VISION OF THE THRONES. Detail: Friar Leo.

Plate 44

THE EXPULSION OF THE DEMONS FROM AREZZO. "How the Blessed Francis saw demons rejoicing over the city of Arezzo and told his companion: 'Go, and in the name of God expel those demons, as our Lord himself has ordered you to do, by shouting from the gate.' And as the friar, obeying Francis, shouted, the demons fled and all was quiet." (See also plates 45–46.)

Plate 45

THE EXPULSION OF THE DEMONS FROM AREZZO. Detail: Friar Sylvester shouting at the demons.

Plate 46

THE EXPULSION OF THE DEMONS FROM AREZZO. Detail: view of the city.

Color Plate I

THE MIRACLE AT GRECCIO. Detail of plate 49.

Plate 47

THE ORDEAL BY FIRE. "How his faith in Christ made him offer to go through the ordeal of fire together with the false priests of the Sultan of Babylon, but none would follow him through the flames and the priests were all put to shame and fled."

Plate 48

ST FRANCIS IN ECSTASY. "One day, as the Blessed Francis was ardently praying, the friars saw him kneeling in a cloud and raised from the ground with his arms outstretched."

Plate 49

THE MIRACLE AT GRECCIO. "How the Blessed Francis, to celebrate Christmas, arranged for a Crib, representing the Adoration of the Shepherds, to be prepared at (the castle of) Greccio. He asked for hay nd for an ass and an ox to be brought there, and preached upon the birth of the poor King. And while he prayed a knight saw that the Divine Child had taken the place of the one laid there by the Saint." (See also plates 50–51 and color plate I.)

Plate 50
THE MIRACLE AT GRECCIO. Detail: rear view of the Crucifix.

Plate 51
THE MIRACLE AT GRECCIO. Detail: the Priest.

Plate 52
THE MIRACLE OF THE SPRING. "As the Blessed Francis went up a hill riding the ass of a poor sick man, and as the man begged for water to quench his thirst, he made the water spring from a rock. Water had never been there before, nor was it ever seen again." (See also plates 53–54 and color plate II).

Plate 53
THE MIRACLE OF THE SPRING. Detail: two friars and the ass.

Plate 54
THE MIRACLE OF THE SPRING. Detail: the thirsting man.

Plate 55
ST FRANCIS PREACHING TO THE BIRDS. Detail: the birds listening to the preaching Saint. (See also plate 56.)

Plate 56
ST FRANCIS PREACHING TO THE BIRDS. "As the Blessed Francis was on his way to Bevagna, he preached to many birds and those creatures did joyfully stretch their necks, open their beaks, stroke his cowl; and all this was seen by his companions who waited by the roadside."

Plate 57
THE DEATH OF THE KNIGHT OF CELANO. "How the Blessed Franc is asked the Lord to save the soul of a Knight of Celano who, as the devout man he was, had invited him to a repast; after the Knight had confessed and made arrangements for his household, and while his guests sat at table to eat, he promptly gave up the soul and found peace in the bosom of God." (See also plates 58–59.)

Plate 58
THE DEATH OF THE KNIGHT OF CELANO. Detail: head of St Francis.

Plate 59
THE DEATH OF THE KNIGHT OF CELANO. Detail: weeping woman.

Plate 60
ST FRANCIS PREACHING BEFORE HONORIUS III. "How the Blessed Francis preached so devoutedly and effectively before Pope Honorius III and his Cardinals that they clearly understood that what he spoke were not learned words of human wisdom but words inspired by God." (See also plate 61.)

Plate 61
ST FRANCIS PREACHING BEFORE HONORIUS III. Detail: head of a papal assistant.

Plate 62
THE APPARITION AT ARLES. "How, whilst Blessed Antony was preaching to the Chapter at Arles about the Title of the Cross, suddenly the Blessed Francis, who was bodily absent, appeared with arms outstretched and in the act of benediction. This was seen by Frate Monaldo, and all the others drew great comfort from it."

Color Plate II

THE MIRACLE OF THE SPRING. Detail of plate 52.

Plate 63

ST FRANCIS RECEIVING THE STIGMATA. "How, as he prayed on the slope of Mount Vernia, the Blessed Francis saw the Savior in the form of a crucified Seraph, and was impressed miraculously on his hands, feet and on his right side with the Stigmata of the Cross, as suffered by our Lord Jesus Christ." (See also plates 64–65.)

Plate 64

ST FRANCIS RECEIVING THE STIGMATA. Detail: the Chapel.

Plate 65

ST FRANCIS RECEIVING THE STIGMATA. Detail: praying Saint.

Plate 66

ST FRANCIS ASCENDING TO HEAVEN. "How, when the Blessed Francis departed this world, a friar saw his soul, in the form of a shining star, ascending to Heaven." (See also plate 67.)

Plate 67

ST FRANCIS ASCENDING TO HEAVEN. Detail: kneeling friar.

Plate 68

THE APPARITIONS TO THE BISHOP AND TO FRIAR AUGUSTINE. The fresco illustrates two episodes which took place at the very moment of the Saint's death: the apparition to Frate Agostino, who was lying ill on Mount Gargano, and that to Guido, Bishop of Assisi: "The friar, who had fallen ill in the land of his labors and had long since lost his speech, suddenly cried: 'Wait for me, Father, for I am coming with you,' whereupon he died and followed his holy father. Furthermore, as the Bishop was journeying on the mount of San Michele Arcangelo, he saw the Blessed Francis who was saying: 'At this moment I am going to my Maker.' And at that moment the Saint was found dead."

Plate 69

THE TESTING OF THE STIGMATA. After the Saint's death news of the Stigmata went round, and many friars and laymen converged upon Assisi to make sure of "that which had caused them great surprise." "As St Francis was lying dead in the Portiuncula cell a scholar and doctor of Assisi, called Geronimo, went and touched the nails, the hands, feet and the side of the Saint with his own hands." (See also plates 70–71.)

Plate 70

THE TESTING OF THE STIGMATA. Detail: a spectator.

Plate 71

THE TESTING OF THE STIGMATA. Detail: painted Madonna.

Plate 72

THE LAMENT OF THE POOR CLARES. "The crowd that had congregated with tree branches and candles, bore the sacred body, adorned with the celestial gems (of the Stigmata), to the city of Assisi, and there they showed it to the Blessed Clara and the other holy virgins." (See also plates 73–74.)

Plate 73

THE LAMENT OF THE POOR CLARES. Detail: two nuns.

Plate 74

THE LAMENT OF THE POOR CLARES. Detail: boy upon a tree.

Plate 75

THE CANONIZATION OF ST FRANCIS. "How the Holy Pope (Gregory IX) came in person to the city of Assisi, examined closely the miracles and, on the advice of his friars, canonized Francis and inscribed him among the Saints."

Plate 76

THE APPARITION TO GREGORY IX. "As the Holy Pope Gregory was doubtful about the wound in the Saint's side, the Blessed Francis appeared to him in a dream and said: 'Give me an empty vial.' And when he had given it to him he saw it being filled with blood from the wound." (See also plate 77.)

Plate 77

THE APPARITION TO GREGORY IX. Detail: St Francis bares his side to show the wound.

Plate 78

BONIFACE VIII PROCLAIMING THE JUBILEE. *Fresco, 110 × 110. Rome, Basilica of St John Lateran.* This is the only remaining fragment of the central and upper part of a great fresco depicting Pope Boniface, between a clerk and a dignitary, traditionally identified as Cardinal Caetani, giving the blessing from the Lateran Loggia after the clerk has read the bull proclaiming the Jubilee. The Loggia, as stated by Panvinio (1570), was erected under Boniface and called *Thalamum* or *Pulpitum Bonifacii.* The remaining fragment of the fresco was detached in 1586 when the Loggia was demolished to make place for a new Lateran Palace designed by Domenico Fontana, and moved to the cloister. A general idea of the complete picture can be had from a drawing in the Ambrosiana Library in Milan which shows (as noted by C. Mitchell in *Journal of the* *Warburg and Courtauld Institutes,* 1951) that the composition was inspired by the *Prize Giving after the Chariot Races* on the obelisk of Theodosius in Constantinople. Early historians do not report on these wall paintings, but Roman scholars of the sixteenth and seventeenth century mention them as the work of Cimabue. Only later were they definitely attributed to Giotto. The fragment, entirely disfigured by age, cracks and repaintings, was restored as well as it could possibly be in 1952 by the Italian Central Institute of Restorations.

It is now generally accepted that it was painted by Giotto in 1300. (Meiss, however, rejects both this fresco and *The Legend of St Francis* as the master's work.) What is disputed, however, is the measure of Giotto's direct participation in the execution. It would appear that he availed himself of many assistants and that—so far as this fragment is concerned—his hand is recognizable only in the head of Cardinal Caetani, at the right of the Pope (plate 79). In our opinion, though, the Cardinal's head is rather weaker than similar figures on the left wall of San Francesco at Assisi —painted, we believe, by Giotto— and is therefore partly due to an assistant. But the fact remains that this fragment is extremely important in that it confirms beyond any possibility of error both the attribution to Giotto of *The Legend of St Francis* and its date of execution before 1300. (See also plate 79.)

Color Plate III

THE MEETING AT THE GOLDEN GATE. Detail of plate 96.

Plate 79

BONIFACE VIII PROCLAIMING THE JUBILEE. Detail: head of Cardinal Francesco Caetani (?).

Plate 80

VIRGIN AND CHILD ENTHRONED. *Panel, 180 × 90. Florence, Church of San Giorgio alla Costa.* A "panel" by Giotto in San Giorgio was mentioned by Ghiberti and by later writers. This Madonna, unfortunately damaged and mutilated (see its graphic reconstruction in *Corpus*, III, Vol. VI, 1956, by R. Offner), was attributed by Offner himself (1927) to a Giottesque artist known as the "Master of St Cecilia." This view was shared by Toesca. The attribution to Giotto was due to Oertel (1937), who dated the panel early 1300, after Assisi and Rome, and before Padua. Oertel also noted the extensive collaboration of assistants.

The authorship of Giotto is now accepted only by Longhi, Bauch, Gnudi, Battisti and me, while Offner, rectifying his first impressions, assigns the panel to the "Master of the *Crucifix* of Santa Maria Novella." The time is variously established between the very early date of Longhi, who believes the panel to be previous to or simultaneous with the *Crucifix* in Santa Maria Novella, that of Oertel in *c.* 1301–3, and the intermediate one of Gnudi who favors a date immediately before the *Legend of St Francis,* therefore about 1296. This is a difficult problem because, while the archaic organization of the picture, and the angels of the Roman school, so reminiscent of the "Master of St Cecilia," belong to the thirteenth century, the heads of the Virgin and Child seem to prefigure clearly the Ognissanti *Madonna and Child in Glory* (plate 185) of about 1310. It would not seem absurd to infer that Giotto executed this panel at two different periods, but only a much desirable cleaning operation could establish the validity of this assumption. (See also plate 81.)

Plate 81

VIRGIN AND CHILD ENTHRONED. Detail: the center.

Plate 82

THE BADIA POLYPTYCH. *Panel, 91 × 340. Florence, Museo dell'Opera di Santa Croce.* The panel consists of five figures: at the center the Virgin and Child; at the right St Peter and St Benedict; at the left St Nicholas and St John the Evangelist. As Ugo Procacci has proved, the polyptych comes from the main altar of the Badia Church in Florence. Ghiberti and others after him assigned it to Giotto. In the fifteenth century the Seraphs were added inside each pinnacle by Jacopo d'Antonio (1451). The first modern critic to ascribe it definitely to Giotto was Thode (1885), but only Suida, Fabriczy, Beenken, Coletti and—partially—Longhi accepted the attribution. Most scholars called it a "workshop-Giotto" (Oertel, Salmi) or saw it as the work of one pupil (Sirén, Volbach, Rintelen, Van Marle, Berenson, Offner, Brandi, Toesca). Judgment was not helped by surface injuries and repaints. The pro-Giotto critics thought it generally to be a late work of about 1330 with the exception of Procacci, for whom it was executed in the master's youth, and Longhi, who dated it early fourteenth century. Despite many irreparable abrasions, recent cleaning has shown the high quality of the execution which, in our opinion too, belongs to the period between Assisi and Padua. (See also plates 83–85.)

Plate 83

THE BADIA POLYPTYCH. Detail: St Peter (right).

Plate 83

THE BADIA POLYPTYCH. Detail: St Benedict (left).

Plate 84
THE BADIA POLYPTYCH. Detail:
St John the Evangelist.

Plate 85
THE BADIA POLYPTYCH. Detail:
the Virgin and Child.

THE FRESCOES

IN THE ARENA CHAPEL

(Plates 86–178)

These very famous frescoes by Giotto cover the only nave of the Scrovegni Chapel (generally called the Arena Chapel) in the Church of the Madonna della Carità or Church of the Annunziata in Padua. The themes depicted are the Life of Christ up to the Pentecost and the events leading up to His birth (*Stories of SS Joachim, and Anne and the Virgin*). The cycle ends with *The Last Judgment*, portraying Heaven and Hell. (See plan on page 56.)

This vast material is distributed in a triple course along the nave's two walls, upon the triumphal arch and on the portal wall in the following manner: the cycle begins on the upper course of the right wall, on the side of the triumphal arch, with six *Stories of Joachim and Anne*, from *The Expulsion of Joachim from the Temple* to *The Meeting at the Golden Gate* (see plates 86–97); it continues at the same level on the opposite wall, from the entrance, with six *Stories of the Virgin*, from the *Birth* to *The Virgin's Return Home* (plates 98–105). Two pictures of the *Annunciation* follow on the sides of the triumphal arch; they are surmounted by the "Celestial Prologue" in which God the Father entrusts the Archangel Gabriel with the message to Mary (plates 106–107). The central part of this, showing *God the Father*, is a panel inserted in the fresco. On the right side of the arch, under the

Annunciate Virgin (plate 108), we can admire *The Visitation*. Thus ends the "prehistory."

On the middle course of the right wall, still on the side of the arch, the *Life of Christ* begins with *The Nativity*; four other stories follow till we come to *The Massacre of the Innocents* (plates 110–119); the narration proceeds on the opposite wall with six stories, from *Christ among the Elders* to the *Expulsion of the Money-Changers from the Temple* (plates 120–128). The difference in numbers between the frescoes on the upper and middle courses is due to the fact that the building is lighted by six windows piercing the side to the right of the portal. The stories from the *Life of Christ* previous to the Passion end with *The Hiring of Judas*, on the left side of the triumphal arch (plate 129). The cycle now moves to the lower course of the right wall, with five stories of the Passion from *The Last Supper* to *The Flagellation* (plates 130–139), and continues on the opposite wall with the last six episodes from *The Road to Calvary* to *The Pentecost* (plates 140–152).

On the triumphal arch, under *The Hiring of Judas* and *The Visitation*, there are two interiors, devoid of figures (plate 154), also called *coretti*. In each of them is a burning lantern symbolizing "the light which guides man to virtue and the light which saves from vice" (Crowe and Cavalcaselle). The skirting along the walls

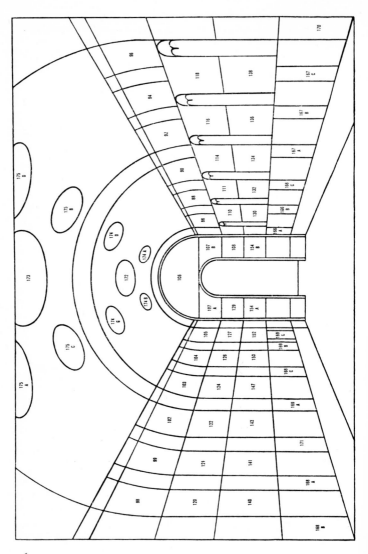

is painted to imitate marble and in its intervals are portrayed the allegories of the *Seven Virtues* (right wall) —see plates 166–171—and of the *Seven Vices* (left wall). Each virtue faces the corresponding vice. With the exception of *Justice and Injustice*, complemented by bas-relief illustrations of their meaning, all the allegories are represented by a single figure.

The stories upon the two walls of the nave are all enclosed in beautiful painted ornaments (see plates 176–178), interrupted at intervals by medallion framings with subjects from the Old Testament and busts of saints. The chapel vault is crossed by three false arches: one, above the triumphal arch, is decorated with figures of angels and saints; the other two, spanning the center and the portal wall, show a series of crowned saints, probably prophets. The field of the vault is blue and starred, adorned with medallions of *Christ* (plate 172), of the Prophets, one of whom is *St John the Baptist* (plate 174) and of the *Virgin* (plate 173).

The entrance wall is entirely covered by *The Last Judgment*, portraying Heaven and Hell (plates 155–165). At the foot of the fresco, on the left of the Cross, Enrico Scrovegni is seen offering his chapel to the Virgin (plate 161).

One can easily see what a rigorous iconographic program must have governed Giotto's work in this chapel.

That he painted the decorations is confirmed in the first place by a coherent tradition going back to his contemporaries, Riccobaldo Ferrarese and Francesco da Barberino. The date can be derived only approximately from the study of documents. One learns that in the year 1300 Enrico degli Scrovegni acquired the Arena site in order to build there a palace and a chapel. The purchase was authorized by Bishop Ottobono dei Pazzi, who died on March 31, 1302. The laying of the chapel's foundation stone—or the site's consecration—took place in 1303 and in March 1304 (Battisti) or 1305 the chapel was dedicated to the Virgin. The term *ante quem* for Giotto's frescoes, as understood from Riccobaldo and Barberino, should be 1312–1313. Considering the magnitude of the work it seems doubtful that, as generally assumed, it was finished in 1305 or 1306. Gnudi (1959) is probably correct in believing that Giotto was called to Padua not by Scrovegni but by the Franciscans and that before attending to the chapel he worked at the lost frescoes in the chapter of Sant' Antonio. Therefore, Gnudi argues, the Scrovegni paintings could have been executed after 1305, more precisely between 1309 and 1310. Gnudi also denies that a protest of 1305 (January 9) by the Eremitani friars—because Scrovegni, by having a bell-tower built beside the chapel, was misusing the Bishop's authority to erect a private chapel—contains any mention of the frescoes. This, however, does not invalidate in the least the possibility that work in the chapel had begun, and the figure of an Eremitano friar in *The Last Judgment*—in the group of the dedication of the chapel to Mary—can only imply that the decoration of the portal wall was started some time after January 9, 1305—when Scrovegni had reached an agreement with the Order.

It is probable, on the other hand, that the *fresco* for the chapel had been planned by wealthy Scrovegni from the moment he decided to erect it and that Giotto began to paint its walls from 1304. Work—Gnudi admits—gives the impression of having progressed rapidly and could have been completed in two or three years. There is no good reason for rejecting the theory that, by the end of 1304, Giotto had finished painting at least the first series of the *Stories of Christ*.

In fact the theory becomes necessary if one accepts that the boy climbing a tree in *The Entry into Jerusalem* (plate 126) was copied by a pupil of Giotto in *The Lament of the Poor Clares* in Assisi, where it has no iconographic function. As *The Lament of the Poor Clares* is stylistically close to *St Francis Being Honored by a Simple Man* (plate 26) it is unlikely to have been painted after 1305.

In conclusion, though Giotto may well have been called to Padua by the Franciscans in 1303, the traditionally accepted date for the Arena frescoes of 1304–1306—and later with regard to *The Last Judgment*—is still the most probable. In fact, it could even be considered proved after Meiss, in 1960, was able to shift back to 1306–7 in the Chapel of St Nicholas in the Lower Church at Assisi, by an anonymous Giottesque, the style of which presupposes the Arena frescoes, especially the *Allegories* in the skirting.

The internal chronology has been disputed. Recently Battisti accepted the theory of Romdahl, Arslan and Baumgart that there is a marked stylistic difference between the "prehistory" compositions in the upper tier and the *Stories of Christ* in the middle and lower courses, leading to the assumption that the upper frescoes were painted later, contrary to the established practice of working downwards. Battisti in fact believes that the order was as follows: *The Last Judgment* (1304), *Stories of Christ* (largely before January 1305) and *Stories of Joachim and the Virgin* (between January 1305 and March

1306). The argument runs that Giotto's *The Last Judgment* is derived, both stylistically and iconographically, from Cavallini's similar painting in Santa Cecilia in Rome, and that the model of the chapel presented to the Virgin in the *Dedication* (plate 161) shows a projecting transept, as originally planned. Therefore, the critic argues, the fresco was finished before January 1305 (the Eremitanis' protest having caused Scrovegni to reduce the chapel's scale). To this one may object that, in the first place, a similarity of scheme to Cavallini's *Judgment* was obviously suggested by the subject itself and that the autograph parts of Giotto's work reveal a softer blending of *chiaroscuro* and color and a gentler treatment of form than the other frescoes in the chapel, such as the master developed in his later works. So far as the *Dedication* scene is concerned, one can say that the same argument is used by Gnudi to claim that the chapel's design was altered just before its completion. Both theories carry the same weight. At any rate considerations of style induce us to prefer a later date for this fresco.

The autograph parts are the figures of *Christ* (plate 157), of the Virgin and Saints who escort her, the *Dedication* scene and a few other details.

The two *coretti* or secret chapels (plate 154) on the sides of the triumphal arch under the scenes of *The Hiring of Judas* and of the *Visitation* have been the subject of special comment by Weigelt, Fiocco, Toesca, Longhi, Gioseffi and Gnudi: these interiors represent Giotto's most daring anticipation of Brunelleschi's type of perspective, in that they are not only correctly designed perspectively but are also referred to a single point of view at the center of the chapel. The triumphal arch (plate 153) fails to fit coherently with the wall. Reasonably, Gnudi thinks that its position was decided at an advanced stage in the building, when instead of a small, rounded apse— as originally planned—the present large apse was designed, with two simulated side-chapels, to resemble a transept. Of these chapels only the one on the left, adjoining the former palace, was actually erected. The one at the right is visible in the model presented to the Virgin in *The Last Judgment*.

Though he worked by no means alone, Giotto made use of fewer assistants here than at Assisi. Other hands are discernible in some *Stories of the Virgin*, in *The Entry into Jerusalem*, in *The Last Supper*, in *The Procession to Calvary*, in some of the *Allegories* upon the skirting, in most of *The Last Judgment* and in the vaults, medallions and feigned arches. The master, however, exercised complete control over his assistants, coordinated each aspect of the work and imposed the mark of his personality in every part of the chapel.

Measurements: the Scrovegni Chapel is 2926 in length, 848 in width and 1280 in height (to the uppermost point in the vaulting). The lateral frescoes are approximately 185; *The Mission to Gabriel* (plate 106) is about 215 in height; the two frescoes on the triumphal arch (plates 108 and 129) are approximately 15 × 14, the *Allegories of Vices and Virtues* on plates 166–170 are 12 × 60; the others are squares of 55; the ornamental partitions between frescoes are approximately 40 in width; the medallions on the vault on plates 172–173 have a diameter of over 1 m.; the diameter of the others is less than 80 cms.; the great fresco of *The Last Judgment* is approximately 10 × 8.40 meters.

Plate 86

THE EXPULSION OF JOACHIM FROM THE TEMPLE. This and the following episodes in this cycle illustrate the narrative in James's *Protoevangelion* and in parts of the Apocryphae. Joachim goes to the temple with an offering but is turned away by Ruben because of his marriage to Anne. Both he and his wife are now aged and have no children. (See also plate 87.)

Plate 87

THE EXPULSION OF JOACHIM FROM THE TEMPLE. Detail: Ruben and Joachim.

Plate 88

JOACHIM RETIRES TO THE SHEEP-FOLD. He retires in sorrow to the mountains, among his shepherds, and lives in penance. (See also plate 89.)

Plate 89

JOACHIM RETIRES TO THE SHEEP-FOLD. Detail: two shepherds.

Plate 90

THE ANNUNCIATION TO ST ANNE. The angel tells Anne that she shall give birth to a child. (See also plate 91.)

Plate 91

THE ANNUNCIATION TO ST ANNE Detail: spinning servant.

Plate 92

THE SACRIFICE OF JOACHIM. In the desert where he has withdrawn, Joachim makes a sacrifice to God. (See also plate 93.)

Plate 93

THE SACRIFICE OF JOACHIM. Detail: the Angel.

Color Plate IV
THE ADORATION OF THE MAGI. Detail of plate 111.

Plate 94
JOACHIM'S DREAM. An angel appears to him in a dream and bids him go to Jerusalem where, by the Golden Gate, he shall find his wife. (See also plate 95.)

Plate 95
JOACHIM'S DREAM. Detail: the sleeping Joachim.

Plate 96
THE MEETING AT THE GOLDEN GATE. After a long separation Joachim and Anne meet by the Golden Gate at Jerusalem. (See also plate 97 and color plate III.)

Plate 97
THE MEETING AT THE GOLDEN GATE. Detail: a bystander.

Plate 98
THE BIRTH OF MARY.

Plate 99
THE PRESENTATION OF THE VIRGIN. (See also plates 100–101.)

Plate 100
THE PRESENTATION OF THE VIRGIN. Detail: the Virgin and St Anne.

Plate 101
THE PRESENTATION OF THE VIRGIN. Detail: two spectators.

Plate 102
THE RODS ARE BROUGHT TO THE HIGH PRIEST. Each of Mary's suitors presents the priest with a rod. The one whose rod shall blossom will be chosen as her spouse.

Plate 103
THE PRAYER FOR THE BLOSSOM-ING OF THE RODS.

Plate 104
THE MARRIAGE OF THE VIRGIN. The rod presented by Joseph has blossomed and a dove has alighted upon it. The betrothal now takes place.

Plate 105
THE VIRGIN'S RETURN HOME. Escorted by seven virgins Mary returns to her parents' home in Galilee.

Plate 106
THE MISSION TO GABRIEL AND ANNUNCIATION. At the bidding of God the Father the Archangel visits Mary and announces to her that soon she will bear a divine Child. In the lower compartments: the *Annunciation*. (See also plate 107.)

Plate 107
Details of the two frescoes of the *Annunciation*: the Archangel Gabriel and the Annunciate Virgin.

Plate 108
THE VISITATION. (See also plate 109.) From this fresco to the end of the cycle the episodes follow the Gospel narrative.

Plate 109
THE VISITATION. Detail: head of the Virgin.

Plate 110
THE NATIVITY. (See also plate 112.)

Plate 111
THE ADORATION OF THE MAGI. (See also plate 113 and color plate IV.)

Plate 112
THE NATIVITY. Detail: Virgin and Child.

Plate 113
THE ADORATION OF THE MAGI. Detail: heads of the Virgin and of St Joseph.

LOCATION OF PAINTINGS

AMSTERDAM

GOUDSTIKKER COLLECTION
St Francis (attribution).
St John the Baptist (attribution).

ASSISI

LOWER CHURCH OF SAN
FRANCESCO
Franciscan Allegories (attribution).
Stories of Mary Magdalene (plate 235–237; attribution).

UPPER CHURCH OF SAN
FRANCESCO
Biblical Stories (plates 1–19 and 230–233; the frescoes in the second group are attributions).
Medallions (plates 24–25).
The Legend of St Francis (plates 26–77 and color plates I and II).

FIUMI COLLECTION
Two Busts of Apostles (attribution).

BERLIN

STAATLICHES MUSEEN
The Death of the Virgin (plates 218–221.
The Crucifixion (plate 254; attribution).

BOLOGNA

PINACOTECA NAZIONALE
Virgin and Child Enthroned with Four Saints (plates 245–246; attribution).

BOSTON

ISABELLA STEWART GARDNER
MUSEUM
The Presentation of Christ in the Temple (plate 239; attribution).

BOVILLE ERNICA (FROSINONE)

CHURCH OF SAN PIETRO IS-
PANO
Angel in Mosaic (plate 179a).

BRUSSELS

STOCLET COLLECTION
The Crucifixion (attribution).
The Nativity (attribution).

CAMBRIDGE (MASSA-CHUSETTS)

FOGG ART MUSEUM
St Francis Receiving the Stigmata (attribution).

CHÂALIS (FRANCE)

MUSÉE JACQUEMART-ANDRÉ
St John the Evangelist (plate 224).
St Lawrence (plate 225).

FLORENCE

BASILICA OF SANTA CROCE
(BARDI CHAPEL)
Stories from the Life of St Francis (plates 196–215).
St Clare (plate 216).
St Ludovic of Toulouse (plate 217).

BASILICA OF SANTA CROCE (BARONCELLI CHAPEL)
The Coronation of the Virgin (plates 247–248; attribution).

BASILICA OF SANTA CROCE (PERUZZI CHAPEL)
Stories of the Two St Johns (plates 191–195 and color plate VII).

CHURCH OF OGNISSANTI
Crucifix (attribution).

CHURCH OF SAN FELICE
Crucifix (attribution).

CHURCH OF SAN GIORGIO ALLA COSTA
Virgin and Child Enthroned (plates 80–81).

CHURCH OF SAN MARCO
Crucifix (attribution).

CHURCH OF SANTA MARIA NOVELLA
Crucifix (plate 20).

UFFIZI GALLERY
Madonna and Child in Glory (plates 185–189 and color plate VI).

PRIVATE COLLECTION
Christ in the Act of Blessing (attribution).

MUSEO DELL' OPERA DI SANTA CROCE
The Badia Polyptych (plates 82–85).

HORNE MUSEUM
St Stephen (plate 222 and color plate VIII.)

PALAZZO DEL PODESTA
The Last Judgment (attribution).
Stories from the Life of Mary Magdalene (attribution).

BARDINI COLLECTION
St Benedict (attribution).

BERENSON COLLECTION
A Franciscan Saint (plate 234; attribution).
The Deposition (plate 242; attribution).
The Crucifixion (attribution).

LONDON

NATIONAL GALLERY
The Pentecost (plate 244; attribution).

ROTHMERE COLLECTION
The Coronation of the Virgin (attribution).

JEKYLL COLLECTION (formerly)
The Redeemer (plate 181).

MUNICH

ALTE PINAKOTHEK
The Last Supper (plate 240; attribution).
The Crucifixion (plate 241; attribution).
The Descent to Limbo (plate 243; attribution).

NEW YORK

METROPOLITAN MUSEUM OF ART
The Adoration of the Magi (plate 238; attribution).

WILDENSTEIN COLLECTION
Virgin and Child Enthroned with Saints and Virtues (plate 256; attribution).

PADUA

CHAPTER OF SANT'ANTONIO
St Francis Receiving the Stigmata (attribution).
The Martyrdom of One Hundred Saints (attribution).

ARENA CHAPEL
Stories from the Lives of the Virgin and Christ (plates 86–153 and color plates III, IV and V).

The Secret Chapels (plate 154).
The Last Judgment (plates 155–165).
Allegories of Virtues and Vices (plates 166–171).
Medallions in the Vaulting (plates 172–175).
Ornamental Bands (plates 176–178).
Crucifix (plates 182–184).

PARIS

LOUVRE
St Francis Receiving the Stigmata (attribution).

STERN COLLECTION
Two Angels (attribution).

PRIVATE COLLECTION
St Paul with Twelve Worshippers (attribution).

RIMINI

TEMPIO MALATESTIANO
Crucifix (plate 180).

BASILICA OF ST JOHN LATERAN
Boniface VIII Proclaiming the Jubilee (plates 78–79).

ROME (See also VATICAN CITY)

BASILICA OF SANTA MARIA MAGGIORE
Medallions with Prophets and *The Eternal Father in the Act of Blessing* (plates 226–229; attribution).

MUSEO PETRIANO
Angel in Mosaic (plate 179b).

SAN DIEGO (CALIFORNIA)

FINE ARTS GALLERY
The Eternal Father and Angels (plate 249; attribution).

STRASBOURG

MUSÉES MUNICIPAUX
The Crucifixion (plate 255; attribution).

VATICAN CITY

BASILICA OF ST PETER
Navicella (mosaic entirely reconstructed).

MUSEO PETRIANO
Angel in Mosaic (plate 179b).

PINACOTECA VATICANA
The Stefaneschi Triptych (plates 250–253; attribution).

WASHINGTON D.C.

NATIONAL GALLERY OF ART
Madonna and Child (plate 223).

REPRODUCTIONS

ACKNOWLEDGEMENT FOR PLATES

Bencini and Sansoni, Florence: plates 1–19, 24–77, 230–233; *Anderson, Rome:* plates 20–23, 80, 81, 86–105, 107–152, 155–178, 180, 182, 184–186, 188, 190–195, 220–222, 234, 238, 240–243, 246–248, 254; *Istituto Centrale del Restauro, Rome:* plates 78, 79; *Gabinetto Fotographico della Sovrintendenza alle Gallerie, Florence:* plates 82–85, 218, 219; *Alinari, Florence:* (the photographs of the Bardi frescoes are from a new edition, following the restoration of those works) 106, 153, 154, 179, 183, 196–214, 216, 217, 235–237, 251–253; *Brogi, Florence:* plates 187, 189, 215; *National Gallery of Art, Washington:* plate 223; *Bulloz, Parigi:* plates 224, 225; *Archivio Fotographico Gallerie e Musei Vaticani:* plates 226–229, 250; *Isabella Stewart Gardner Museum, Boston:* plate 239; *National Gallery, London:* plates 244, 245; *Fine Arts Gallery, San Diego:* plate 249; *Musées Municipaux, Strasbourg:* plate 255; *Wildenstein, New York:* plate 256; plate 181 is reproduced from the magazine *Paragone.*

The plans on pages 44 and 56 are by Roberto Roveroni. The reconstruction of the Navicella fresco on page 84 is reproduced from a photograph supplied by Alinari, Florence.

Plate I. ISAAC BLESSING JACOB, Assisi, Upper Church of San
Francesco

Plate 2. *Detail of plate 1*

Plate 3. ISAAC REJECTING ESAU, Assisi, Upper Church of San
Francesco

Plate 4. *Detail of plate 3*

Plate 5. *Detail of plate 3*

Plate 6. THE BAPTISM OF CHRIST, Assisi, Upper Church of San Francesco

Plate 7. *Detail of plate 6*

Plate 8. CHRIST AMONG THE ELDERS, Assisi, Upper Church of
San Francesco

Plate 9. *Detail of plate 8*

Plate 10. THE SLAYING OF ABEL, Assisi, Upper Church of San
Francesco

Plate 11. THE LAMENTATION, Assisi, Upper Church of San Francesco

Plate 12. *Detail of plate 11*

Plate 13. *Detail of plate 11*

Plate 14. *Detail of plate 11*

Plate 15. THE RESURRECTION, Assisi, Upper Church of San
Francesco

Plate 16. JOSEPH IS SOLD BY HIS BRETHREN, Assisi, Upper Church
of San Francesco

Plate 17. *Detail of plate 16*

Plate 18. THE FINDING OF THE CUP IN BENJAMIN'S SACK, Assisi,
Upper Church of San Francesco

Plate 19. *Detail of plate 18*

Plate 20. CRUCIFIX, Florence, Santa Maria Novella

Plate 21. *Detail of plate 20*

Plate 22. *Detail of plate 20*

Plate 23. *Detail of plate 20*

Plate 24. MEDALLION WITH THE VIRGIN AND CHILD, Assisi,
Upper Church of San Francesco

Plate 25. MEDALLIONS WITH ANGELS, Assisi, Upper Church of
San Francesco

Plate 26. ST FRANCIS BEING HONORED BY A SIMPLE MAN, Assisi,
Upper Church of San Francesco

Plate 27. ST FRANCIS GIVING HIS MANTLE TO A POOR KNIGHT,
Assisi, Upper Church of San Francesco

Plate 28. *Detail of plate 27*

Plate 29. *Detail of plate 27*

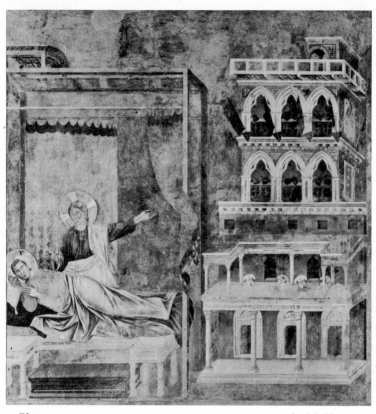

Plate 30. THE DREAM OF THE PALACE AND ARMS, Assisi, Upper
Church of San Francesco

Plate 31. THE CRUCIFIX OF ST DAMIAN SPEAKS TO ST FRANCIS, Assisi, Upper Church of San Francesco

Plate 32. ST FRANCIS RENOUNCING THE WORLD, Assisi, Upper
Church of San Francesco

Plate 33. *Detail of plate 32*

Plate 34. *Detail of plate 32*

Plate 35. THE DREAM OF POPE INNOCENT III, Assisi, Upper Church
of San Francesco

Plate 36. *Detail of plate 35*

Plate 37. *Detail of plate 35*

Plate 38. THE SANCTIONING OF THE RULE, Assisi, Upper Church of
San Francesco

Plate 39. *Detail of plate 38*

Plate 40. THE VISION OF THE FIERY CHARIOT, Assisi, Upper
Church of San Francesco

Plate 41. *Detail of plate 40*

Plate 42. THE VISION OF THE THRONES, Assisi, Upper Church of
San Francesco

Plate 43. *Detail of plate 42*

Plate 44. THE EXPULSION OF THE DEMONS FROM AREZZO, Assisi,
Upper Church of San Francesco

Plate 45. *Detail of plate 44*

Plate 46. *Detail of plate 44*

THE MIRACLE AT GRECCIO
Assisi, Upper Church of San Francesco
(detail of plate 49)

Plate 113. *Detail of plate 111*

Plate 112. *Detail of plate 110*

Plate III. THE ADORATION OF THE MAGI, Padua, Arena Chapel

Plate 110. THE NATIVITY, Padua, Arena Chapel

Plate 109. *Detail of plate 108*

Plate 108. THE VISITATION, Padua, Arena Chapel

Plate 107. *Detail of plate 106*

Plate 106. THE MISSION TO GABRIEL AND ANNUNCIATION, Padua Arena Chapel

Plate 105. THE VIRGIN'S RETURN HOME, Padua, Arena Chapel

Plate 104. THE MARRIAGE OF THE VIRGIN, Padua, Arena Chapel

Plate 103. THE PRAYER FOR THE BLOSSOMING OF THE RODS,
Padua, Arena Chapel

Plate 102. THE RODS ARE BROUGHT TO THE HIGH PRIEST, Padua,
Arena Chapel

Plate 101. *Detail of plate 99*

Plate 100. *Detail of plate 99*

Plate 99. THE PRESENTATION OF THE VIRGIN, Padua, Arena Chapel

Plate 98. THE BIRTH OF MARY, Padua, Arena Chapel

Plate 97. *Detail of plate 96*

Plate 96. THE MEETING AT THE GOLDEN GATE, Padua, Arena Chapel

Plate 95. *Detail of plate 94*

THE ADORATION OF THE MAGI
Padua, Arena Chapel
(*detail of plate III*)

Plate 94. JOACHIM'S DREAM, Padua, Arena Chapel

Plate 93. *Detail of plate 92*

Plate 92. THE SACRIFICE OF JOACHIM, Padua, Arena Chapel

Plate 91. *Detail of plate 90*

Plate 90. THE ANNUNCIATION TO ST ANNE, Padua, Arena Chapel

Plate 89. *Detail of plate 88*

Plate 88. JOACHIM RETIRES TO THE SHEEPFOLD, Padua, Arena
Chapel

Plate 87. *Detail of plate 86*

Plate 48. ST FRANCIS IN ECSTASY, Assisi, Upper Church of San
Francesco

Plate 47. THE ORDEAL BY FIRE, Assisi, Upper Church of San
Francesco

Plate 86. THE EXPULSION OF JOACHIM FROM THE TEMPLE,
Padua, Arena Chapel

Plate 85. *Detail of plate 82*

Plate 84. *Detail of plate 82*

Plate 83. *Details of plate 82*

Plate 82. THE BADIA POLYPTYCH, Florence, Museo dell'Opera di
Santa Croce

Plate 81. *Detail of plate 80*

Plate 80. VIRGIN AND CHILD ENTHRONED, Florence, Church of
San Giorgio alla Costa

Plate 79. *Detail of plate 78*

THE MEETING AT THE GOLDEN GATE
Padua, Arena Chapel
(*detail of plate 96*)

Plate 78. BONIFACE VIII PROCLAIMING THE JUBILEE, Rome,
Basilica of St John Lateran

Plate 77. *Detail of plate 76*

Plate 76. THE APPARITION TO GREGORY IX, Assisi, Upper Church
of San Francesco

Plate 75. THE CANONIZATION OF ST FRANCIS, Assisi, Upper
Church of San Francesco

Plate 74. *Detail of plate 72*

Plate 73. *Detail of plate 72*

Plate 72. THE LAMENT OF THE POOR CLARES, Assisi, Upper Church
of San Francesco

Plate 71. *Detail of plate 69*

Plate 70. *Detail of plate 69*

Plate 69. THE TESTING OF THE STIGMATA, Assisi, Upper Church
of San Francesco

Plate 68. THE APPARITIONS TO THE BISHOP AND TO FRIAR
AUGUSTINE, Assisi, Upper Church of San Francesco

Plate 67. *Detail of plate 66*

Plate 66. ST FRANCIS ASCENDING TO HEAVEN, Assisi, Upper
Church of San Francesco

Plate 65. *Detail of plate 63*

Plate 64. *Detail of plate 63*

Plate 63. ST FRANCIS RECEIVING THE STIGMATA, Assisi, Upper
Church of San Francesco

THE MIRACLE OF THE SPRING
Assisi, Upper Church of San Francesco
(detail of plate 52)

Plate 62. THE APPARITION AT ARLES, Assisi, Upper Church of
San Francesco

Plate 61. *Detail of plate 60*

Plate 60. ST FRANCIS PREACHING BEFORE HONORIUS III, Assisi,
Upper Church of San Francesco

Plate 59. *Detail of plate 57*

Plate 58. *Detail of plate 57*

Plate 57. THE DEATH OF THE KNIGHT OF CELANO, Assisi, Upper
Church of San Francesco

Plate 56. *Detail of plate 55*

Plate 55. ST FRANCIS PREACHING TO THE BIRDS, Assisi, Upper
Church of San Francesco

Plate 54. *Detail of plate 52*

Plate 53. *Detail of plate 52*

Plate 52. THE MIRACLE OF THE SPRING, Assisi, Upper Church of
San Francesco

Plate 51. *Detail of plate 49*

Plate 50. *Detail of plate 49*

Plate 49. THE MIRACLE AT GRECCIO, Assisi, Upper Church of
San Francesco